THE PERFECTIONIST'S GUIDE TO KNOWING WHEN IT'S GOOD ENOUGH

SIMPLE STRATEGIES TO HELP YOU STOP OVERANALYZING, FOCUS ON WHAT TRULY MATTERS, MOVE ON TO THE NEXT STEP, AND ACTUALLY GET THINGS DONE

SPENCER FOSTER

HMS PUBLISHING

For Jacob

CONTENTS

INTRODUCTION

"Perfect is the enemy of good."

VOLTAIRE

If you could make anything in your life perfect, what would it be? A perfect mind? A perfect body? A perfect career?

The search for perfect provides an escape. The fantasy we chase in our minds is a distraction from certain mentally unpleasant feelings.

Ultimately, however, this desire for perfection creates more stress, high standards, and feelings of disappointment. One could say perfect is also the enemy of *good enough.*

The yearning to be perfect is an urge many share, influenced by our surroundings, upbringing, and societal expectations. Navigating the challenges that perfectionism brings is not a struggle for the weak. Like many, I am a perfectionist myself, an obstacle bestowed upon me from the unfolding of random events and influences. Despite the challenges presented, I've managed to surpass some of the inner control perfectionism can have on a mindset. The journey of overcoming these struggles inspired me to share this guidance with those experiencing similar setbacks.

GOOD ENOUGH

Perfectionism is something I've struggled with for as long as I can remember. My focus on a particular task would become so fixated on one small aspect that I would completely lose all concept of time. Before I knew it, several hours would pass, and I had only an hour or two left in the shift to complete the entire project. On many occasions, I had to tell my boss that I didn't finish and would have to resume the task the next day. For the most part, I didn't get into *too* much trouble because my managers knew that I completed every job to perfection. However, when a deadline was drawing near, I could tell when they were less than thrilled with my inability to let something be *good enough.*

It wasn't until the last few years that I realized just how negatively impactful perfectionism was in my life. These habits had gotten to the point where they were impacting my finances, and I knew I had to make a change.

My breaking point came in more recent years after a friend of mine offered me a side job. She owned several rental homes, and one had recently become vacant. She asked me to fix it up to make it ready for new renters. She knew of my tendencies and was careful to stress that she wasn't selling the house, so it didn't have to be pretty; it just had to be functional. Any potential renters would not be concerned with minor blemishes and would most likely cause plenty of their own damage while living there.

She told me that she would cover all material costs, and since I had a tendency to overdo things, she would pay me a flat fee of $1,000 rather than an hourly rate. This way, I would have to prioritize what was truly important—because the longer the job took me, the less it would be worth my while.

After doing a walkthrough of the house, I noted that it needed some drywall repairs, the floors all needed a deep cleaning, and the whole house would benefit from a fresh coat of paint, but it didn't look too bad overall. I determined that if I could complete the project in 40 hours of work, I would make around $25 an hour, a reasonable hourly wage I could live with.

As I started work, the inevitable happened: I caught myself spending *too much* time on things that *did not* matter. It didn't take long to realize that completing the job in 40 hours was unlikely, and then it became a question of just how low my hourly rate would be once I was done.

I did my best to remind myself that things didn't have to be perfect—they only had to be *good enough*. This is very easy to say but very hard to do. There were many times when I would catch myself scraping off the drywall mud I had just applied because it wasn't perfectly smooth. Then, I'd reapply it only to scrape it off again... and again... and again, until I would yell out loud and scold myself, saying, "It's good enough! Leave it alone!"

I would then make good progress for a few minutes until, once again, I would catch myself scraping and reapplying the mud. Perfectionism was something I could notice for a brief moment and avoid; but eventually, I fell back into the mindset of these deeply engrained habits.

When the project was finally finished, it had taken me 117 hours to complete. That equated to a whopping $8.55 per hour. At least I hadn't fallen below minimum wage, but it was definitely not worth my time.

That's when I knew I needed to get my perfectionism under control and learn to embrace what it means to be *good enough*.

PERFECTIONISM MANAGEMENT

Freedom from these perfectionist struggles is possible. The perfectionist mindset tells us that nothing is ever satisfying enough. Even when extreme standards are met, new ones are instantly created in the search for perfection.

Like me, you've probably realized that perfectionism has negatively impacted your life, and you're tired of the stress that these habits bring on. You miss out on opportunities, procrastinate on your goals, and see your dreams pass by as time continues. This can lead to isolation from others and avoidance of necessary risks and challenges that can help us live a happier life.

The management of perfectionism starts by identifying where and how these thoughts developed, as this can lessen their impact and increase awareness of automatic habits. After, the addition of self-reflection, certain tips, and other practical methods can help mediate your thoughts.

Perfectionists are on the rise. Now more than ever, teens and adults feel the pressure to live up to physical, career, financial, and other high-to-reach standards. The effects range from small habits to big life decisions, and that can chip away at our quality of life.

By changing habits, setting goals, and creating valuable boundaries, you can face the fears that drive perfectionism. This habit isn't a life sentence. You have the tools to work through debilitating thoughts. With practice and some realistic exercises, you can develop self-empowerment skills and apply them to your life.

CHAPTER 1
PERFECTIONISM EXPLORED

P erfectionism drives an urge to reach high standards, which might seem like a good thing. It's great to push yourself and to want great results! However, studies show that perfectionism is often a weakness in the workplace (Breidenthal et al., 2018).

To overcome an issue, you must first understand it at the core.

Perfectionism has been something that can feel passive at times, but it has been actively affecting your life. You can recognize habits and tendencies, but you might not exactly know what that is doing to your life to the fullest extent.

For example, consider the difference between a broken leg and simple leg pain. If you were to injure yourself and break your leg, you would go to the doctor and get it set in a cast, knowing what the cause of the issue is, what the issue is doing to your body, and what is going to be needed to recover and overcome these tendencies.

If you simply had leg pain, you would have to recognize all of the actual symptoms that are coming along with that leg pain. Is it just achy pain? Are you also experiencing back pain because of this? Is the leg pain getting to the point where it's impacting your day-to-day life? Does it only occur at night? Does it only hurt when you're walking, or is it a constant ache and pain? The doctor would need all of these little symptoms to help them fully comprehend and diagnose what is causing that leg pain. Then, once you do get a diagnosis—for example, something like fibromyalgia— you would want to understand what that condition is at the core to fully comprehend the way it's going to continue to impact your life and what necessary steps you can take to overcome it.

Now, it is time for you to grasp perfectionism in a full sense, so you are the one who is in control rather than letting these habits and tendencies be the ones that hold power over you. Anybody can use a car or a plane to travel. However, if that car breaks down or if that plane stops working correctly, you call an expert to help fix it to ensure that you can safely travel once again.

You must become an expert on perfectionism so you can troubleshoot the issues in your life. Just like leg pain, you know what it feels like to struggle with perfectionism; however, what does that look like in your individual life?

If you are like me, then you have likely hit a point where you recognize that this is a problem that can't be ignored anymore. Perfectionism first started in a mild form. For example, I noticed that I was the type of person who would get very annoyed when a picture or poster was not straight on the wall. Most people strive to hang things straight and use levelers or other tools to ensure this happens. However, most of us don't notice every single picture that's out of place everywhere we go. I found myself staring at pictures on the walls of restaurants. I would see one that was crooked, and before I knew it, all I was thinking about was how much I wanted to get up and fix that picture. I had mentally lost all concept of the conversation that my dining companion was trying to have with me. Wanting a picture to be straight on the wall is normal. Being so distracted by an imperfect picture that you're missing out on valuable moments with others has a much more detrimental impact.

These small habits don't heavily damage your life, but they are gateway thoughts that can lead to bigger issues. There are more mid-range forms of perfectionism, like constantly redoing completely adequate things just because of a few minor imperfections. Again, this is something that can be very common and normal on a small scale; wanting to redo things is necessary at times. However, you might be struggling with perfectionism to the point that you are always redoing things, ultimately getting the same results each time.

Perfectionism can even get to the point where it is debilitating and negatively impacts your personal or romantic relationships, finances, and career. This involves something like completely shutting down and failing to make an attempt because of a slight flaw. On a personal level, I can recall trying new hobbies, not being very good at them the first time, and then never trying again. I've played games with friends where I wasn't very good, causing me to lose interest and avoid going back later. Being a perfectionist means wanting to get perfect results every time; but in reality, it requires a lot of growth and time to see actual change and positive results.

Perfectionism causes us to overanalyze to the point that it becomes difficult to make a decision and focus on the things in life that matter the most, and overcoming perfectionism requires us to take a look at the foundation of what builds these tendencies.

PERFECTIONISM VERSUS OCD

It's also important to note that there is a difference between being a perfectionist and being somebody who struggles with obsessive-compulsive disorder (OCD). In our society, we've watered down symptoms of OCD and made it seem more like some sort of personality quirk than what it is: a debilitating mental condition.

OCD is a much more harmful mental health condition. It is similar to perfectionism in ways but takes those similarities to a much more intense level. Obsessive-compulsive disorder involves rituals and habits that are unrelated to perfectionism. For example, a perfectionist might be a student who is hard on themselves to get perfect grades; therefore, they spend excessive amounts of time studying and redoing their work. Somebody who's struggling with OCD might get to the point where they're actively self-harming when they get bad grades. They might have rituals, like skin picking or hair pulling, that are completely unrelated to schoolwork. A perfectionist might want a meticulously clean kitchen, but someone who struggles with OCD might spend three hours washing the same few dishes, feeling like each attempt just isn't right. We all like to make sure our house is locked and secure when we go to sleep at night, but someone with OCD might lock and unlock their door 10 or more times, struggling to sleep because of the debilitating fear that someone will break in.

Not everyone who has OCD self-harms, so it can be confusing to know the difference at first. However, it's important to recognize that unless you have a specific diagnosis, it's best not to treat perfectionism as an obsessive-compulsive disorder. In some cases, it can be considered insensitive to refer to your perfectionism as OCD. Perfectionism is more of a mental habit and frustration, whereas OCD is a clinically debilitating disorder.

That's not to say that if you have extreme perfectionism, you don't have intense challenges in your life. However, it's important to note that in some cases, if you believe you are struggling with obsessive-compulsive disorder, you might need medical help. Whether it's through one-on-one counseling or prescribed medication, professionals trained in OCD can ensure you get the right treatment plan.

Even if you are struggling with extreme forms of perfectionism, you can often still help yourself work through some of these issues on your own by noticing patterns and taking initiative. If you avoid medical treatment for certain mental health conditions, it can make them worse. Consider seeking professional help ASAP if you struggle with one or more of the following symptoms:

- thoughts or acts of self-harm
- thoughts of suicide or suicidal ideations
- disordered eating, like binge eating or periods of extreme restriction
- impulsive habits that are negatively impacting finances (like gambling or excessive shopping)
- impulsive habits that are putting your safety at risk
- struggles with addiction or excessive use of harmful substances like drugs or alcohol

Even if you are unsure of whether you are struggling with OCD or perfectionism, a second opinion never hurts! You can overcome perfectionist habits, but don't be afraid to ask for help.

TYPES OF PERFECTIONISM

Perfectionism can be seen as a phobia (MacDonald, 2011). This phobia is one in which making mistakes is the greatest fear. There are many reasons why this fear exists, and recognizing that fear can help determine the type of perfectionism you've been struggling with. You might struggle with elements of all types of perfectionism, or one singular type might resonate with you. By understanding the type of perfectionism you've been struggling with, you can make a more targeted action plan to reduce these symptoms.

There are thought to be three components of perfectionism: self-oriented perfectionism, other-oriented perfectionism, and socially-prescribed perfectionism (Taylor, 2021).

These three types can help describe some of the motives and core fears that we have behind perfectionism. The first type is self-oriented perfectionism. This is when you are hyper-fixated on yourself and your flaws. Personally, this is one of the types that I struggle with the most, as I fixate on the work I do and the intense pressure I put on my performance. If you struggle with self-oriented perfectionism, then you are caught up in what you're doing and how that is going to be perceived by other people. You aren't as concerned with what others are doing; instead, you create your standards mentally and focus on them to the point that it causes stress or anxiety.

The second type is other-oriented perfectionism. This is when those high standards are placed on other people rather than yourself. You will notice this for managers, parents, and other people who might be in positions of leadership. It's easy to place standards on somebody else without having to meet those standards yourself. This leads to having a more judgmental mindset, where you focus on the flaws other people have and their inadequacies. This can be the most damaging to your relationships, as you might become resentful or overly critical, even to the point that the other person fears your potential judgment.

You might struggle with socially-prescribed perfectionism. This is when you are very fearful of the judgment of other people. You want to be perfect because you want to be perceived as perfect. You might notice that when you are alone or doing something that you enjoy, you might not have as many perfectionist tendencies. However, if you are going out to socialize or displaying your work for other people, that might be when more of those perfectionist tendencies set in.

You can have one of these types or some combination. I find that for me, my self-oriented perfectionism is often because of socially-prescribed perfectionism. They both combine with each other to create excessive stress, perpetuating a cycle that can be hard to break free from.

In addition to these three types of perfectionism, you can also categorize your traits between being adaptive and maladaptive perfectionism. Adaptive is when you can take those traits and use them for good. This serves as a reminder that perfectionism isn't inherently something that will damage your life. It can be what helps drive you to be detail-oriented, focused, and thorough with your work. However, when it becomes maladaptive, that is when it becomes counterintuitive and damages you more than having no type of perfectionism at all.

Some of the traits of perfectionists who are struggling include unrealistic standards, fear of failure, low self-esteem, high criticism, and having a result-focused mindset. As a perfectionist, it's easy to create unrealistic standards because you have this idealized image in your head of how you want things to turn out. Getting those results is much more challenging.

In our minds, we're creating a fantasy. It's kind of like using special effects in a movie. When watching a superhero movie, there might be a 10-second clip of someone flying, making that image appear clearly on screen. But going about that can be incredibly challenging. You have to have stunt coordinators, people who are trained in this type of thing, editors, and other special effects to get there.

In your mind, you have the image of *perfect*. You have the result. You have the scene completed in your head. However, now you have to take all of those little steps to get there, which can be incredibly difficult. When you fail to reach those high standards, you end up blaming yourself and feeling bad about your abilities. In reality, nobody would be capable of reaching those high standards because they are simply not possible.

You cannot make somebody fly. You can only make it look like they are flying, and even this takes a lot of effort. It takes only a second to envision someone flying in your mind.

This example serves to exhibit how it's easy to picture exactly what you want, but getting there is hard, and when you fail to reach that perfect image, it results in low self-esteem and self-deprecation.

Perfectionists also tend to be extremely results-focused, meaning only the end goal is important. The actual process of getting there is often rushed through as quickly as possible. It also becomes a very egregious and unsatisfying process. This can end up leading to procrastination because you want to avoid any pain and suffering that you have to endure to get to the things you want.

All of these factors can make us extremely self-critical to the point that we become our own biggest bullies. As you start to unpack some of the side effects, habits, and types of perfectionism, you can begin the process of transforming these tendencies into something more valuable and productive in your life.

LABEL SYMPTOMS

Being a perfectionist isn't something to get rid of but to maintain at a realistic level. Perfectionism can even be seen as a good thing at times, as it provides "conscientiousness, endurance, satisfaction with life, and the ability to cope with adversity" (MacDonald, 2011).

Acknowledging the way these habits have been harming us is the important first step. Once you do this, you can then turn some of them around to become more productive. For example, your extreme attention to flaws can become a higher attention to detail.

Other types of symptoms you might be experiencing are:

- distraction or lack of focus
- anxiety
- low self-esteem
- feeling lethargic or burnt out
- excessive regret and rumination

Perfectionism causes us to waste time by going over and over things that don't require that much energy from us. This has a detrimental impact on life, and all of the combined symptoms above can lead to missed opportunities. Consistent "failure" (or perceived failure) breaks us down over time, leading to exhaustion and constant disappointment.

Another very impactful symptom of perfectionism is procrastination. Globally, at least one in five adults struggle with procrastination (*Why You Put Things Off*, n.d.). Many driving factors behind procrastination can be related to perfectionism. Often, people equate procrastination with laziness, creating the sense that someone is avoiding a task because they simply don't feel like doing it. This is certainly the case at times! However, those who struggle with procrastination might find that they are so afraid of failure that they avoid the tasks that require their attention altogether.

All of these things combined can lead to low-quality work and late or absent submissions, which only exacerbate stress. When we feel bad about ourselves or inadequate, it can cause us to withdraw from others and isolate ourselves to avoid judgment. This can lead to relationship strain and loneliness.

The first action step is to label the way perfectionism has specifically impacted your life:

- Finish this sentence: Perfectionism causes me to...

Repeat that sentence as many times as necessary until you feel as though you've covered the symptoms of anxiety in your life. Examples include:

- Perfectionism causes me to fixate on work too much, making my managers upset that work is often late.
- Perfectionism causes me to skip social events because I'm afraid of what others think of me.
- Perfectionism causes me to feel excess stress over the results, leading me to become distracted with anxiety.
- Perfectionism causes me to give up easily when I don't get things right the first time.
- Perfectionism causes me to judge myself and even others very harshly, making it easier to isolate and feel like an outcast.
- Perfectionism causes me to miss deadlines, leading to even more missed opportunities.
- Perfectionism causes me to believe that if I'm not perfect, there's no point in even bothering to try.

Writing these thoughts down on paper helps you keep track of the way your life has been impacted while also providing you with a point of reference to return to as you make progress. I highly encourage journaling throughout this process so you have a space to store your thoughts, reactions, questions, and emotions as you navigate through the book. It doesn't have to be a physical journal either. Use a notes app on your phone or a preferred digital document system to help you easily jot down thoughts as they come to you.

Creating awareness of the impact of perfectionism is the crucial first step in overcoming these thought patterns.

TRACK IMPACT AND EFFECTS

Perfectionism negatively impacts our lives because it can create an avoidance tendency. You will notice this when you struggle to stay on schedule and get things done because you are focused on going over the tasks or projects repeatedly.

When we participate in perfectionist rituals, it can cause us to set ourselves up for failure. I know firsthand how frustrating it is to create hard-to-reach standards and then fail to meet them over and over again.

Perfectionism takes away our ability to appreciate the moment because we focus on the future and the results. When we struggle to fully enjoy our time, even moments of relaxation become stressful and riddled with panicked thoughts.

Reducing perfectionist tendencies by utilizing the exercises throughout the book will help you create a strong action plan to overcome your fears, triggers, and stressors.

The next action step in understanding perfectionism is to track the impact it has had and what effects this has led to. To do this, start by identifying the main motivations of perfectionism. Recall the three types discussed:

1. self-oriented perfectionism
2. other-oriented perfectionism
3. socially-prescribed perfectionism

What are the biggest driving motivations behind the urge to be a perfectionist? Identifying what motivates you will make it easier to overcome perfectionist habits. Do you want to please others? Are you distracting from an inner fear? Do you place pressure on others to get the best results? Finish this sentence:

- I feel the need to be perfect because...

You can write this below the previous sentences, but keep it simple, as we'll dive deeper into the roots of perfectionism in Chapter 2. Examples include:

- I feel the need to be perfect because I'm afraid of what others think.
- I feel the need to be perfect because I don't want to fail in my career.

- I feel the need to be perfect because I want to impress my colleagues.

For the next two weeks, track habits that align with perfectionist tendencies by writing them down when you notice them happening. This can be a simple list, like:

- 9 a.m.: I changed my outfit twice before heading to work.
- 11 a.m.: I spent 20 minutes reading a short email, feeling anxious about saying the perfect thing in my reply.
- 12:30 p.m.: I worked through my lunch break, redoing a project that was almost done because I was afraid to turn it in.

You can look at the time and notice if there was anything that might have triggered it. For example, you might notice your perfectionism is the worst at night as you anxiously anticipate the next day.

These are small examples of little habits throughout the day that can contribute to a bigger mindset. At the end of each day, make a note of how you feel. After a couple of weeks, you will have a better gauge of just how negatively impactful these habits have been in your life.

CREATE GOALS

Having an idea of what you want to achieve provides a substantial focal point for growth. As a perfectionist, you likely have many goals as it is! These are also likely very hard-to-reach goals and are based on standards that are not so easily achieved. To create goals, follow these steps:

1. Create a realistic goal. Is this a reasonable goal? Is it based on real experiences? Just because it is the best possible outcome does not mean it is something you can realistically achieve.
2. Create specific goals. The goal of wanting to save money is great, but break it down into more substantial steps, like starting with saving $100 and increasing that amount over time.
3. Create goals that have time limits. Perfectionists tend to disregard time when they start working, as the focus changes to fixate on the results. Sticking to a time limit can keep you on track. I have found that I maintain better focus and get more done when I have a deadline.

Start by making a goal for your perfectionist tendencies. These can be small, like:

- go a day without saying anything mean to yourself
- finish a project in the original timeframe allotted
- finish something the first time without going back and changing it a bunch

After you have had some success with these small goals, you can begin to make larger life goals that are specific and relevant to your personal preferences, like a career or financial goal. Once you start achieving goals, you then have proof that you are successful, productive, and capable of making great change. Even when you are afraid of the results, you can look back on your accomplishments and think to yourself, *I was able to achieve that, so I know I can do this.*

FOSTER REFLECTION

Reflection tactics are important for self-awareness, self-growth, and self-empowerment. The great thing about reflection is that it doesn't require expensive tools, specific locations, or even a lot of time. You can self-reflect anywhere you are, at any time. In addition, it can be helpful to create self-reflection periods, like going on a quick walk around your block after dinner every night or spending an extra 15 minutes reflecting in the morning before you get ready for work. There are a few important rules to keep in mind when self-reflecting:

- Go into it without bias. Sometimes, we reflect in a way that we want to prove something specific, and this can cloud our judgment. For example, I've had times when I felt like a failure, so my brain would try to investigate past experiences for evidence that this was true. This is more like self-deprecation or negative rumination than healthy self-reflection.
- Go into it without judgment. Sometimes, our perfectionist tendencies are rooted in problematic thoughts. For example, you might be hard on yourself when it comes to looks. You might call yourself ugly or other mean names. Rather than

harshly judging yourself, try to remain objective and view these thoughts or phrases in a reflective light. If you make a mistake, you might think to yourself, *Why did I do something so stupid?* Instead, try to remain neutral and ask yourself, *I wonder what led me to make that decision?*

Healthy reflection will make it easier to notice habits and thoughts and find a way to turn them into something more productive and substantial.

CHAPTER 2
GETTING TO THE ROOT

When I was in elementary school, I was a chubby kid. This made me an easy target for classic bullies looking for low-hanging fruit. I was constantly picked on, had no friends, and had very low self-esteem. It was hard for me to socialize and do well in school because I was constantly afraid of what my peers might be thinking. I often experienced stress over when the next time somebody would pick on me might be. Trying anything new was entirely out of the question. I didn't want to set myself up for even more embarrassment or give my peers fuel for jokes at my expense.

I felt isolated and alone, and this certainly had an impact on my development. I was afraid of doing anything wrong. Not only was there the chance that somebody else might say something to me, but even if they didn't, I still had their voice in my head, picking apart my every move. The voices of my bullies carried with me through middle school and high school; even as an adult, some of their words lingered in my mind.

What this resulted in overtime was my desire to make sure that I did absolutely everything *perfectly*. If I did it perfectly, then there was no room left for criticism. In addition, I thrived off of praise. I was so used to hearing such negative things from other people that when somebody offered me praise, it felt like sunshine on a cloudy day.

However, my desperation to reach perfect standards didn't necessarily result in those perfect standards I set out to achieve in the first place. In fact, it often ended in less-than-perfect work because I would miss assignments completely or at least have to ask for additional time to get them done. While my final results usually were close to perfect, at that point, I would end up receiving less praise because my bosses and teachers were already a little frustrated that I needed so much time to complete my projects.

The criticism and lack of praise I received only exacerbated the perfectionism that was rooted in my childhood. I was constantly getting triggered and always left dealing with the side effects that the stress of perfectionism caused.

Perfectionism didn't stay isolated to one part of life, either. It would spread into my personal life and began to affect relationships. The voices in my head had become meaner than anything an elementary school bully told me as a child. In turn, I became my own biggest critic, making it difficult to get anything done at all.

Coming to this realization was vital for me to overcome some of the fears, causes, and triggers that were perpetuating the constant cycle of anxiety. My desperation for perfection didn't exist just so I could get praise. It was so I could heal some of the wounds left open from childhood bullying. I didn't only want to satisfy my peers and superiors —I also wanted to help that inner child realize that he was not what his bullies told him he was.

Getting to the root of perfectionism will help you understand the core fears that fuel these tendencies. The perfectionist habits and thoughts that are in the driver's seat of perfectionism often end up veering us off the road to success and, instead, take us down different paths away from our goal. Often, these paths lead back to our childhood.

SEEDS OF PERFECTIONISM

In many cases, seeds are planted in our brains over time that create a system of weeds, and the only way to ensure a weed doesn't grow back is by removing it at the root. You can cover up weeds. You can spray them and temporarily kill them. However, finding the source and digging it out will ensure they never come back. This is hard for many because it is messy and requires that you get your hands a little dirty.

For some, perfectionism comes from a fear of failure, and for others, it is a fear of criticism. Both of these fears tap into our basic human need for acceptance. We are group animals and prefer to travel in packs. Unlike loner animals, like certain felines or reptiles, we have a dependency on other people. Humans have evolved to have a diverse diet over time, and this requires a collection of hunting for protein and gathering plants for nutrients. This is a lot of work to do on your own, so we formed groups, tribes, and societies over time to ensure our needs are met. We have the fear of rejection and social ostracization because that means we might not have our basic human needs met. Nowadays, most people can head to a grocery store to collect the necessary foods for a diverse diet, but we still have the basic human urges wired into us. This is why rejection can sting so much —it cuts deeply into our inherent survival skills.

During our developmental years, we have these basic human instincts and desires wired into us, but we are even more dependent on others to ensure those needs are met. As children, we want love and compassion from our parents. We want acceptance, recognition, and praise from peers and teachers. Not getting that can certainly impact development.

That's not to say that rejection means we won't survive or that we're set up for failure. However, tracing our roots back to how we were raised can help provide more insight into some of the reasons we might be struggling to break these thought patterns as adults.

Parenting styles are very influential on perfectionists. In fact, having a perfectionist parent can cause damage to a child's well-being when tendencies go unmanaged (Morin, 2021). Consider if you learned this high-standard-seeking behavior from a parent. I knew someone in college who was a straight-A student. He aced every assignment, quiz, and project and completed them better than most in his class. However, every time he would talk to his parents, they weren't very excited about the good grades. Their baseline expectations were for him to be perfect; therefore, when he was perfect, he didn't receive much praise. It was the basic behavior that was expected of him.

This is an example of perfectionist parents. Those who are always expecting perfection are extremely hard to satisfy. Making our parents or caregivers proud is a big part of childhood development, so never receiving that praise can make us strive especially hard to try and get it.

In addition, social pressures are intensely influential on a perfectionist mind. Take the media, for example. From the hair on our heads to the shoes we wear, there is intense pressure to fit into a specific "look." On top of that, social media has made it easier than ever before to erase flaws and create false images of things that don't even exist. The endless comparison leaves us feeling like we are never good enough, even after editing pictures.

Cultural and belief systems are engrained in our psyche, and breaking free from them can feel nearly impossible. The combination of parenting styles, societies, and our very belief systems creates the recipe for our perspective. At the end of the day, most of us just want praise, recognition, and acceptance, and comprehending this urge as a child was incredibly confusing. When approval was granted, it was then confused for love (*Perfectionism*, n.d.). After learning that praise equaled love, we then spent years seeking praise, never truly fulfilled even when recognition was granted.

What this tells us is that, sometimes, the roots of perfectionism are simply there and are attached to specific personality traits. Since culture and society influence us so heavily, not every perfectionist is going to have a specific trauma that caused their habits, like bullying or an overbearing parent. Accepting that these habits are a part of who we are makes it easier to embrace perfectionism and utilize it in a healthier way.

Because perfectionism intrinsically becomes a part of who we are, it's easy to think that it works! For example, I recall a time when I waited until the last minute to turn in a project. I kept starting and then redoing it, and the deadline popped up in the blink of an eye. Nervous and regretful, I reluctantly showed up to class empty-handed. Luckily for me, the instructor was out sick and sent an email stating that we had the weekend to finish the project. Everyone who had finished showed their dismay, but I relished in the success of my procrastination. I was able to finally finish the project, taking advantage of my second chance. In this case, perfectionism actually worked out in my favor. Unfortunately, most of the time, perfectionism does not work out like this. However, the brain can store these instances of when perfectionism works, using that as justification for more perfectionism in the future.

Perfectionism provides us with a sense of control (Martin, 2015). The future is so unknown. Even when we have a strong idea of how things will likely turn out, there are many factors outside of our control that we have no power over. Perfectionism tricks us into thinking that if we get it *just right*, we can ensure all of those fears we're struggling with will not happen. Even procrastination provides a sense of predictability. You know you can get things done last minute, and you often do, so your mind keeps perpetuating this habit.

Despite us making it this far in life, that doesn't mean we were happy, carefree, or successful. Going forward, it's crucial that we identify the roots, habits, and potential causes of perfectionism to ensure they don't keep coming back.

WRITE A LETTER

Perfectionism can also cause rigid thinking or a lack of creativity (*Perfectionism*, n.d.). Breaking free from perfectionism means exploring your creativity and nourishing your inner passions. As I mentioned in the last chapter, a great way to do this is through writing or journaling. In addition to any other journaling you've done thus far, consider this prompt:

- Write a letter to your past self.

This can help you better understand how your past connects to your present. As you start a conversation with your inner child, you open your mind up to explore some of the past triggers and memories you might've overlooked.

If you have experienced severe trauma in your childhood and find that this is too triggering, try writing a letter to any version of a younger you, even if it is to yourself from last year at this time.

Not all of our habits necessarily lead back to specific childhood experiences, but noticing some of the habits we've collected over time can help us differentiate between what is average behavior, what might be a learned personality trait, and which are cycles we've endured over time.

As you're writing this letter, here are some things to talk to your past self about:

- what successes you've had
- what felt like a failure at the time but turned out to be okay
- what caused you stress as both a child and an adult
- what things caused you stress as a child that don't matter now
- what you were afraid of happening, whether or not it did happen, and what the results of this were
- something that you hoped would happen but didn't and whether or not that was ultimately a good or a bad thing
- any lessons you wish you would've known then that you know now and what it took to learn these lessons

You don't have to write about all of these things, and you can discuss any additional topics that come to mind when writing. This should be a cathartic activity to help you gain greater insight into some of the habits that have rooted themselves into your brain and how they've changed over time.

REWRITE MISTAKES

Think back to a time of regret. Now, rewrite that scenario in the third person from the perspective of someone else who witnessed the failure. This is to help you reframe your "failures." For example, consider how you might struggle with self-confidence and fixate on your flaws. You notice every wrinkle in your face, but can you think of another person whose wrinkles you notice? We often highlight our flaws and disregard our successes. In your journal, recall a time you made a mistake and how a third party might've viewed this. Some examples are below to give you a sense of this activity:

- After moving into a new apartment, Kelsey struggled to pay her rent. After taking some unpaid sick days from work due to stress, she was a few hundred dollars short this month. She ended up having to ask her sister for help, and this was embarrassing and defeating for her. She's always thought of herself as an independent person who can take care of herself, so asking for help made her feel like a failure. Her sister, Rachel, has a much different perspective. She believes that her sister is extremely hard-working. She's constantly surprised at how far Kelsey has been able to make it in life. She worked hard to get where she was in life, and like many, she had a temporary setback. Rachel is so grateful she was able to help Kelsey out to relieve some of her anxiety. Kelsey has helped Rachel out plenty of times in the past, and now Rachel feels great she's been able to repay all of those favors.

- Michael is an athlete who's had record-breaking success at his school. He's a swimmer, and he was able to make it into the state finals, the only representative from his school who was able to do so. He finally gets there, only to get the worst score of all. He feels defeated and has a breakdown in the locker room that his coach, Daniel, witnesses. From Daniel's perspective, he is amazed at how talented Michael is. He knows how hard he is on himself, and while he was excited about Michael making it to state, he was simultaneously concerned at the pressure Michael would feel. Daniel did his best to coach him through and is proud that he even had the opportunity. Daniel feels worse about how upset Michael is rather than being upset about the results of the race.

When we are hard on ourselves, it's sometimes difficult not to assume that everyone else is just as disappointed as we are. However, as long as we do our best and show effort, others are much more likely to be proud, amazed, and inspired by us rather than experiencing feelings of disappointment.

SPARKS OF PERFECTIONISM

In more serious cases of perfectionism, it can spread like a fire, destroying its path. Knowing the sparks of perfectionism can help us prepare for these tendencies to ensure they don't continue to burn through many areas of our lives.

The sparks of perfectionism are like the triggers that get the cycle started. It takes only one small thought to turn into a day of rumination. The cycle begins with an anxiety or stressor after there's an attempt to alleviate the perfectionism, which ultimately results in even more high standards. After that, there's more stress and anxiety, which, again, sparks the desire for more perfectionism.

If you are able to label the biggest sparks that are causing these tendencies, you then know how to prepare for them and prevent the spiral after you have been triggered.

The first place to start is in our society, which, these days, is often perpetuated through social media. If you use different social media platforms like Facebook or Instagram, you might often see your friends, peers, classmates, colleagues, and other individuals in your social circle post about their lives. For the most part, these posts are often very positive. You'll see engagement, wedding, and baby announcements. You'll see people showing off the material things they bought, or they'll display their bodies and appearance in a positive way. People often don't post pictures of themselves with messy hair, stained clothes, and licking the chip dust off their fingers while on their third binge watch of a TV show. People are more likely to post their happy couple photos rather than videos of them fighting with their partner. Parents post their children's achievements and won't as often share that they were in detention for picking on other kids.

This creates a very skewed perspective where we are only seeing everybody else's highlights. Then, we tend to highlight the negative aspects of our own lives because of our perfectionist tendencies. What results is a juxtaposition of our "worst" and everyone else's "best." This comparison leaves us feeling unsatisfied, and that causes us to start blaming ourselves. Social media can perpetuate the idea that what you have is what you earned; therefore, that creates an alternate feeling where what you don't have is also your fault. For example, that classmate who just purchased a house doesn't reveal that their parents gave them the money for the down payment.

We see only bits and pieces of somebody else's life, but those small moments end up looking so bright that they cast our lives into the dark shadows. When we're left alone in the dark, the only person to blame is ourselves, making it harder to find the motivation for positive change.

If you find yourself often struggling with comparison, it's important to take a break from social media. It's also very helpful to limit the types of posts you see. If somebody is constantly posting about the great things in their life, you don't necessarily have to unfollow or block them. Depending on the social media platform, you might be able to limit their posts based on certain social media settings. It's also crucial when you do notice yourself getting triggered by these instances that you stay grounded in reality. Balance it with the likely truth. Remember that somebody else's good life events now don't indicate that you won't have that in the future. Somebody's life might actually just be "perfect"—and that's okay. That doesn't mean your life will never be.

The next spark of perfectionism is criticism or perceived criticism. The thing about a perfectionist mindset is that we're often ready for criticism, and we even unknowingly seek it out. If somebody makes a neutral statement, it's easy to twist that into criticism, even if that's not exactly what they meant. For example, if you show up to a party wearing a new shirt with an intricate pattern, somebody might say, "Wow, that's an interesting shirt!" They didn't say, "That's a cool shirt." They didn't say, "I love your shirt." What they said could go either way. Our perfectionist mind then tells us that they think our shirt is ridiculous or that we don't look that great. They might simply think that it is genuinely an interesting shirt, but our perfectionist mindset causes us to lean on the negative side of things.

In addition, somebody else's praise can sometimes feel like our criticism. If you show up to a party with a friend and somebody tells your friend, "You look great tonight," you might sit there and think to yourself, *Does that mean that I don't look great?* They might just be talking about your friend's new haircut or, perhaps, they recently saw your friend when they *weren't* looking so great.

Somebody else's praise doesn't necessarily mean that you are receiving criticism, but it certainly can feel that way. Since praise is what we are often seeking, it then triggers us to want to seek that approval we see someone else getting, leaving us feeling defeated when we don't.

We also have very intense pressure and standards from academic, social, and professional settings. The standards that we are given often create a baseline, and our perfectionist mindset tells us that we have to go even further above these basic standards. This can be very triggering because, often, our academic or professional standing reflects how successful we feel in our lives. If we are not getting good grades, does that mean we're not going to get a good job? If we are not doing well in our careers, does that mean we're destined for failure?

Going forward, identify the biggest triggers that have been perpetuating perfectionism. What is it that causes you the most stress and anxiety in terms of not being good enough? What are the biggest underlying fears that result in feelings of inadequacy? Being able to identify these triggers can help you take a more realistic and objective standpoint against them, reducing the validity and intensity they have on your life.

EXPLORE YOUR DEEP SUBCONSCIOUS

The brain is a complex organ that we still know very little about. One aspect of the brain that still baffles many is dreams. Dreams can be attached to many spiritualities or even religions. Some people think dreams are spirits sending messages; others think we are traveling to different realities throughout the night. Regardless of what belief system you follow, what we can know for certain is that our dreams can carry deeper messages to help us understand our waking brain.

In fact, one study proved that participants had more ease when solving their waking problems after recording some of their dreams (Summer, 2023). Since perfectionism is so attached to deep, underlying fear, it makes sense that we can find help working through these issues when we tap into the deep subconscious of our minds.

Analyzing dreams is a way to see if there is something deeper your mind might be trying to tell you. Not every symbol or sign necessarily has meaning in your dream. Sometimes, you'll see outrageous things, have interactions with celebrities/movie characters, or a talking animal might even appear. However, if you consistently mark down your dreams, you might notice patterns and recurring themes that provide greater insight into your conscious thoughts.

The first step to a dream journal is to choose your medium. You can use the same journal you've been writing in, but I prefer to have a different one that I can always keep at my bedside. I set it down right next to my alarm clock with a pen. You often forget dreams right away, so it's helpful to have immediate access to write them down.

Next, focus on symbols, people, and emotions you have in your dream. Trying to describe everything you see is challenging and not always necessary. Focus on the main things you remember, as these are likely the most valuable parts. Consider the who/what/where/when of the dream. Examples of some recent dreams I've had that I recorded include:

- I kept finding snakes outside my house that were trying to crawl in through the windows.

- I was flying from rooftop to rooftop and saw a concert happening in the streets below me.
- I was called to present something at work, and my teeth kept falling out.

These are all very common dream themes. Snakes might indicate untrustworthy people. Teeth falling out can show a sign of insecurity. Flying carries many different themes, like independence or even a loss of control.

After you write down your dreams, see if you can interpret them on your own. Afterward, utilize an online dream interpreter or even a book of dream meanings to provide greater insight into what's going on in your head.

SET LIMITS

Setting a time limit is vital to help you reduce perfectionist tendencies. A time limit is the best way for me to get things done. Seeing the countdown of the clock serves as a reminder that I have to keep going, even when it doesn't "feel right." Through my experiences, one of the most important things I've learned is that turning *something* in is better than turning *nothing* in.

Set time limits for non-tasks as well. Use apps on your phone to limit how much time you spend on social media, or consider deleting your accounts for at least a week. A digital detox helps rework perfectionist thoughts.

INTENTIONAL CONFRONTATION

Find a mild trigger and confront it, ensuring it isn't anything too intense so it doesn't have adverse effects. For example, if a mess is triggering, intentionally mess up a small organized space in your house. If social interactions are the most triggering, smile and say hi to a stranger as you pass them in the grocery store. Small instances of exposure can help us get comfortable with imperfection. By pushing yourself through this experience, you can help turn your bully voice into one that cheers you on.

Developing this essential self-compassion will help you get through moments when your brain is telling you that you are not good enough. At the end of the day, we are all humans who make mistakes, and learning to embrace this will ease the urgency of a perfectionist mind.

CHAPTER 3
YOU ARE HUMAN

Humans make mistakes, and we are also prone to experiencing stress as a survival tactic, so learning to view the less-than-enjoyable aspects of life in a new light can make them more tolerable. On a physical level, stress doesn't feel great, so there's an urge to avoid this feeling altogether. When we feel stressed, there's this sense that something might be *wrong*.

In college, I had a roommate with whom I lived for a year, and during that time, we had one class together. This was a basic prerequisite class that everybody had to take. It was a humanities course, and we all needed to complete a project for the end of the year. The project was based on a specific group of people throughout history, and we had to write about their backstories, customs, and so on. The project involved writing a paper and then presenting our research to the class. The grading scale was either pass or fail; it wasn't based on a percentage. All it took to pass the project, *and* the class, was basically our completion of the requirements. Our class was on a Tuesday, and the weekend before was the last weekend before we would all leave for the holidays. It was a very exciting time, and everybody was getting together to celebrate. I had finished a huge portion of the project, but I was still going through it over and over again, making sure that every last detail was perfect. This wasn't even a subject that was necessarily in line with my major or my passions; but every time I had a big presentation like this, I felt incredibly nervous.

My roommate managed to finish his project rather quickly and decided to head out for the weekend. He got together with some friends and spent plenty of time enjoying his freedom now that most of the schoolwork was done. I, on the other hand, spent the entire weekend making sure that every last detail of this project was perfect. I kept going through all of the assignment requirements and rereading the rules to make sure that I was getting everything done correctly. The day of the presentation came, and my submission was planned perfectly. I had every word written down on a notecard. My roommate, however, basically shrugged off this assignment and completed it on his first pass. He jotted down a few notes for talking points and let his confidence do the rest of the work. When he went up to give his presentation, he didn't have many pictures or slides prepared, but he still nailed it. He had moments where the class laughed. The students seemed enthralled by what he was doing. Overall, his presentation was one of the best in the class.

Mine wasn't necessarily bad, but it was pretty rigid and uniform. It was to the point and, for lack of a better term, somewhat basic. Other people had projects that were pretty similar to mine, and the class didn't really seem that interested in what I had put forward.

Both of us ended up passing the project, and both of us got around the same final grade for the class. I had spent my last weekend before leaving for the semester on this project. I missed out on hangout sessions with my friends, as well as much-needed downtime and relaxation periods. My roommate was able to not only get a good grade but also enjoy spending time with his social circle. This experience proved to me that it is not always how much effort you put in that gives you the best results. In fact, sometimes doing things too efficiently creates rigidity, depleting valuable uniqueness that can set you apart from the rest. My roommate went into this project with relaxation and confidence, and I was obsessed with the smallest of details. This showed through in both of our work, and while we each completed the project with a passing grade, ultimately, it's clear that my roommate had a better experience overall.

Learning how to accept things as being *good enough* means embracing the chance of mistakes. Perfection is an obsession with covering all your bases and making sure that every requirement is met. Learning how to embrace imperfection gives you more confidence so you can be creative with the process and actually enjoy the journey rather than being obsessed with only the results.

Embracing imperfection is an important part of overcoming perfectionism.

GETTING COMFORTABLE WITH IMPERFECTION

The urge for perfection is uncomfortable, and some might even describe it as painful. They're not wrong, and I know this feeling all too well. In fact, research suggests that emotional and physical pain are activated in the same brain region (Gillette, 2022).

The amygdala is the region of the brain thought to be responsible for our fight-or-flight response, impulsivity, and decision-making skills (Hof, 2021). Since perfectionism taps into our fears, it then impacts our ability to make decisions. When we are struggling to get work done or feeling deeply insecure, this will create a sense of urgency as our desire to evade these emotions increases. The discomfort of perfectionism then leads us to act impulsively and make poor decisions.

Perfectionism is a collection of feelings and behaviors that cycle through emotional triggers followed by an attempt to alleviate these challenging emotions. By learning how to sit with that discomfort, it becomes easier to work through perfectionism.

The first step of acceptance is to ensure that you withhold any judgment. Judgments create standards (even if you are not explicitly judging yourself.) For example, if you show up to work one day and your coworker has messy hair, you might think to yourself, *Wow, what's wrong with his hair?* Then, the next time you're having a bad day or when the wind ruffles your hair and you look in the mirror, you end up judging yourself in that same way. Our judgments create an inner voice that upholds impossible standards. Often, these standards disregard realistic human error and natural mistakes.

Getting comfortable with imperfection also means that we must learn how to sit with the sensations that come with imperfection and, therefore, not judge those either. For example, emotional pain can feel like physical pain. When you're anxious, you might start to feel your heart race. You might experience back pain or get a headache from the stress. When you notice these sensations, it's important to objectively recognize them. State how you're feeling by saying something like, "I feel like I'm experiencing pain from stress. I don't feel great."

Making a judgment on this pain will make you feel even worse. You might think to yourself, *This is really bad. There's something really wrong with me. I feel really sick.* If you start to make these judgments, it starts to make stress worse, so you're left not only enduring the initial emotional pain, but now you also have even more stress to unpack.

As you are getting comfortable with imperfection, it's crucial to notice connections between some of these types of emotions. If you feel stressed out at work, you can easily bring that stress home. You might get frustrated with your partner or roommate for something small, like forgetting to put their dish in the dishwasher. While your roommate's actions are completely separate from what happened at work, the emotions can connect to each other because we carry those stresses with us throughout the day. Small triggers and annoyances in your personal life might be fueled by stress from your professional life and vice versa.

Being able to make these connections helps increase your emotional awareness so you can recognize when perfectionist tendencies are driving how you feel. As you increase awareness, withhold judgment, and notice your senses, it becomes much easier to practice actually sitting with those imperfections and getting comfortable with mistakes. We are all human beings, which means that we are imperfect by nature. We can only do so much based on our environmental factors and the way we were raised.

Consider something like being an environmentally conscious person. You can make sure to avoid genetically modified foods. You can remove all plastic or similar materials from your life. At the end of the day, you still can't control the air you're breathing or what pollutants might be contaminating the water you're drinking. There is always going to be something that is outside of your control that makes it hard for you to be perfect. We have to accept imperfection or else it creates an all-or-nothing mindset where you might feel like there's no point in trying if you can't reach perfection.

Humans are imperfect. Nature is imperfect, and the world is not a perfect place. Embracing the idea that perfect doesn't even exist in the first place is going to make it easier for you to learn how to sit with uncomfortable perfectionist feelings.

GET MESSY

It's one thing to know that perfection is impossible, but actually feeling and living that lifestyle is much different. To help you get started on the right track, one activity to try is to *get messy*.

The best type of activity for this is something that is physically messy. It should be a complicated process that involves materials that can either be hard to work with or unpredictable in nature. For example, gardening is a great messy activity.

Anyone can garden. If you have an outdoor spot or a small balcony, you can garden. If you have a big windowsill or a sunny spot in your house, you can garden. Anybody can play with the soil, get their hands dirty, and watch as something grows. Plants are also imperfect. You can't determine where a leaf is going to sprout or what direction the plant decides to move in any way. Soil is also very messy and sometimes even has things like bugs or mold in it. Go to your local garden store. Pick out a small plant. Buy a bag of soil and a pot that is a size bigger than the pot the plant came in. Remove the plant from the plastic container that it came in and place it in the pot. One author who has helped me learn some of the basics of gardening is Bruce McCord. He does a great job of explaining the process while providing valuable insight into the horticulture world.

The next part is when things get really messy. You can use gloves if you want, but using your bare hands can also help you experience some of the sensations that the mess can bring on. Reach your hand into the potting mix and feel the soil in your hand. Place the soil on top of the plant, burying the roots and creating stability. Don't pack it down too tight. Once that's done, water the plant and watch as it grows!

The workspace that you're in will likely be messy, and the plant might look a little awkward after you plant it. It's going to take some time for it to grow and stretch out in its new container before it looks its best.

Other types of messy activities include things like cooking. Pick a complex meal that has a lot of ingredients. Doing this can help you learn how to sit through periods when things simply don't feel perfect. Make something that requires getting your hands dirty, like homemade pasta.

Get messy artistically and try something like clay sculpting or finger painting. Both of these activities require that you get your hands physically dirty, so you have to feel the sensation of the mess on your hand as you're working with these materials.

GIVE A COMPLIMENT

As a perfectionist, both giving and receiving compliments might feel pretty uncomfortable. As I mentioned in the last chapter, sometimes another person's praise makes us feel like we're receiving criticism.

At the same time, receiving compliments yourself might feel uncomfortable because you don't believe their validity. If somebody says, "You look great today," when you feel like your hair is a mess and your outfit is mismatched, you're not going to believe them. You might assume that they're simply being nice. I've had times in my life when I struggled with so much insecurity that sometimes I worried the other person was actually making fun of me!

The practice of giving and receiving compliments can make it easier for you to embrace the reality that you *do* have good qualities, even in times when you feel imperfect.

Next time you're interacting with somebody, no matter who it is, give them a compliment. If you are currently home right now with somebody else around you, next time you take a break, go give them a compliment. Compliment their appearance or their intelligence. Compliment something they said or show gratitude for something that they did in the past. If you aren't going to be interacting with somebody you know personally, you can still give a compliment to a stranger.

Next time you go to the coffee shop and order your morning brew, tell the barista you like their hair or their shoes. Compliment the jacket of the person in front of you in line. Of course, you should focus on finding a genuine compliment, but that shouldn't be too difficult. Notice one thing that you like about somebody you see and share this acknowledgment with them.

Seeing them light up will make you feel good and help you recognize that you have value and worth and a positive influence on somebody else's life. Chances are, this person will also compliment you in return because we often feel the urge to do so when somebody gives us praise. This is an added bonus to this exercise because embracing compliments from other people can be a challenge in itself.

LEARNING TO ACCEPT YOURSELF

We have only one body, one brain, and one life. The resistance against ourselves means that time is spent avoiding who we are at the core. Accepting yourself feels uncomfortable, especially when the perfectionist mind can think of so many things to dislike.

A lot of perfectionism comes from an urgency to alleviate the negative feelings we have, like fear, so learning radical acceptance and how to sit with oneself can empower us through moments of perfectionism.

Self-acceptance and self-esteem are two different concepts that are important to understand (Seltzer, 2008). Self-acceptance means embracing who you are unconditionally. Your self-esteem is how you view your worth, which will be influenced by whether or not you are able to foster self-acceptance. Self-acceptance also requires that we embrace who we are, even when others don't.

Acceptance starts with self-awareness and refusal to be resistant to unconditional love. For example, picture a couple, Matt and Michelle. Recently, they welcomed their first child. Like many people who give birth, Michelle's body changed. Over the next few years, she struggled to keep the baby weight off and didn't dress up as often as she used to when she was younger. If Matt unconditionally loves Michelle, he will embrace these changes and still show appreciation and compassion toward her. Conditional love would be based on her looks; therefore, he might feel less attraction and love toward her after she went through these changes. We all deserve someone who loves us unconditionally, and that starts with self-love.

The conditions that we give ourselves are often based on unrealistic standards, making acceptance harder and perpetuating resistance. An inability to show self-acceptance can even increase your brain's stress signals (Pillay, 2016). Perfectionists never feel like anything is good enough because we are often smart, talented individuals. We are detail-oriented and have a great focus on success. However, this constant desire for more will eventually burn us out, depleting all of our energy. The sooner we practice methods of self-acceptance, the sooner we will feel like we are finally good enough.

JUST ONCE

What is your favorite hobby or a craft you enjoy? For this next activity, challenge yourself to create something small, the only rule being that *you are only allowed to make one attempt.* Try picking something that you really only have the option to do once, like decorating a cake, for example. Sure, you could remake the entire cake if you mess up, but that's a lot of work for something you're just going to eat. Consider painting as well, as this is harder to redo. If you force yourself to make an attempt and stick to the first result, you will often find that you are more accepting of yourself than you realize. Redoing things over and over distorts our perception and causes us to lose the reality of the goal we set out to reach in the first place. Repeat this activity whenever you get the opportunity to help you recognize how much better you feel when you learn to embrace your first attempt as being *good enough*.

BODY SCAN

A body scan meditation can help us get used to sitting in the moment, no matter how uncomfortable it may be. To do this, find a comfortable spot and sit in a comfortable position. Ensure your arms and legs aren't crossed, and provide a back and headrest, like by using a pillow. Release all of the tension in your body and notice your pattern of breath. Go through each of these parts of your body and focus on how it feels in the moment. Linger on this part as you breathe in and out. The parts to go through include:

- the top of your head and forehead
- your ears and eyes
- your mouth, nose, and cheeks
- your chin and jaw
- your neck and shoulders
- your arms to your elbows
- your forearms, wrists, and hands
- your chest and upper back
- your abdomen and lower back
- your waist and pelvic region
- your upper thighs
- your knees
- your shins and calves

- your ankles and feet
- the tip of your toes

After you scan from the top to the bottom, reverse the order. Remember to linger there and consider "flexing" this part and then releasing it on days when you are experiencing heightened stress. Some body parts you can't really flex, like your wrists or ankles, but you can tense areas like your shoulders, abdomen, thighs, fingers, and toes. Squeeze these areas and release them as you continue breathing to help redirect your focus and increase comfort at the moment.

CELEBRATE YOURSELF

Think back on a success you've had in the past. Now, take some time to celebrate this instance again, especially if you didn't celebrate yourself in the first place. Was it a graduation? A new job offer? The purchase of a home or car? Even something small like getting a call back for a job you ultimately didn't get is still something to celebrate! Cleaning your house, exercising for 30 minutes, or reworking your resume are all small things that should be celebrated.

In addition, consider this: You reached someone else's perfect already—and they would have celebrated. Why don't you? Noticing your successes provides reassurance that you are capable of great things *and* deserving of the benefits that these successes bring.

CHAPTER 4
A HABIT A DAY

Our emotions, thoughts, and experiences shape the actions and motivations we have throughout the day, so finding small ways to tweak these behaviors will help us work through perfectionism. Many small daily habits reinforce perfectionism, so changing habits in small ways can be very powerful. Perfectionism isn't one quick fix. It's a collection of micro instances that contribute to a debilitating mindset.

The biggest perfectionist habit I have noticed is the habitual nature of my automatic thoughts and reactions. Every time I would get close to the end of a task or make a small mistake, I would have the same type of thoughts. I would be very sarcastic in my mindset and say things to myself like, *Oh great, another failure*; *Surprise! I messed up again*; or *Classic me, always making mistakes.*

These types of phrases were expected and happened without thought. They would contribute to even more negative self-talk at that moment. When I was already feeling bad about myself for procrastinating or making a small mistake, these automatic thoughts would pop in and make it even harder to stay motivated and keep pushing through until the end. There are many automatic little habits throughout the day that have seeped into your routine. The thing about habits is that we often want to wipe them away from our lives. We want to simply snap our fingers and have them gone, but unfortunately, that's not possible. There are many intrinsic factors that make it difficult for us to rework habits. In addition, every time we remove a habit from our life, it leaves an empty space. Our automatic brain wants to fill in that space, so it's easy to revert back to that habit. The key to overcoming perfectionism is not just by erasing it from your life, but by replacing it with more productive habits.

YOUR FILTER SYSTEM

Your habits are driven by your motivations, and your motivating factors are fueled by your emotions. This is why it can be so hard to change habits. They aren't just small actions you take but can actually be deeply embedded into your emotional psyche.

Our perception is a completely subjective experience. Subjectivity refers to how it can change depending on past experiences and personal situations. Perception is what you choose to take in, and that certainly changes over time.

As a child, I was a picky eater. I stuck to the basics, like chicken nuggets and French fries. As an adult, my perception of food has drastically changed, and now I like experimenting with different flavors and cuisines I've never tried before. Even if I think I might not like it, I still try unique foods I've never tasted before. My perception is that we should embrace every opportunity to try something new. As a teenager, I used to not have as much interest in black-and-white movies and preferred newer things that came to theaters. As an adult, my perception is that these movies can be incredibly interesting, especially when they were made in a different time period. These are small examples of how our perception can shift over time.

Our perception dramatically shifts as we age from youthful minds into adults with many more experiences. Perception also shifts simply based on who you are. Even individuals with similar genetics and backgrounds, such as twins, can have completely opposite perceptions. One might perceive the world as being a beautiful and loving place. They're very kind and generous. The other one views the world from a negative perception and isolates themselves from other people because they dislike humanity in general.

Our perception is based on many different factors and will alter our thoughts, emotions, and behaviors. Take, for example, a common and simple product of nature, like a tree. Many different people can have different perceptions of this tree. An arborist first looks at the bare stalks and starts to diagnose what might be wrong with the tree. A woodworker looks at the grain first and notices the intricacies in the trunk of the tree. A forager looks for mushrooms that are growing at the roots and around the bottom of the tree. Our perception is based on our experience and motivation. It is based on what you choose to notice. After, our perception is how we interpret that information. The arborist sees the bare leaves and thinks that this is a bad tree that needs to be cut down. The forager looks at the mushrooms and sees that there is an active ecosystem going on within the soil and believes that this is a great spot to pick mushrooms from. The woodworker sees the tree as a tool and wants to chop it down so they can use it for their own projects.

Our perception is also based on what motivates us to make the next move. The forager realizes that they have plenty of mushrooms at home and there's no need to pick these for their cuisine, so they leave them for other animals. The arborist decides that cutting down the street might be a little bit too dangerous, so they leave it as is. The woodworker starts to calculate the costs of what it would take to chop the tree down to use it for their projects.

As you can see, a perception of something as simple as a tree can be drastically different based on who is looking at it, what they interpret from their perception, and what they choose to do afterward. These small actions and information-processing moments create our habits. Some people have the habit of looking at something and figuring out how they can make use of the tools and supplies they're given. Other people have a habit of wanting to know everything and trying to figure out how things work. Some people have the perception that if it doesn't apply to their personal life, then they simply ignore it, and it doesn't really matter.

The thing about our habits is that they don't have to be *good* —they just have to work. This is why there are certain individuals who wait until the last minute to wake up and only give themselves 10 minutes to get ready for work. They still end up making it on time, even if they're five minutes late a few days a week. Ultimately, though, it still works! They keep their job, so there's really not much motivation to change other than feeling rushed in the morning. However, at night, they want to stay up later and keep watching TV or talking to their friends, so all of a sudden, that motivation doesn't really matter to them.

What happens is that the combination of our perception and our habits creates our truth over time. *The truth* is objective, but *our* truth is our subjective experience. Since we choose what to focus on and what to ignore, we can then start to validate any belief system that we want. This is why you have to *want* to change in order to see change. That person who waits until the last minute to wake up in the morning believes the truth is that as long as they are getting by and keep their job, they don't really have to make a change. Ultimately, if they end up losing their job, then that might motivate them even more to want to make that change. The motivation becomes external since they need a new career. However, as long as something is working, their belief system is going to stay the same because their thoughts start to validate that belief system.

All of these things create a mental filter, which chooses what we take in and what we put out. Changing that filter means changing the way we view our failures and successes in general. As a perfectionist, it's important for you to change your perception so you know how to move past some of the debilitating parts of your day-to-day life and use them for good. This means rethinking the way you see failure so it can actually become a success. If you look at a failure or a past mistake and view it with the perception of how you can improve next time or turn it into a learning experience, then it becomes a much more valuable instance.

When you see value in failure, it's a lot less scary to experience later on. In fact, you might actually seek out mistakes and failures, such as criticism or feedback, when you are not afraid because you understand how valuable it can be and how much it'll help you improve.

To help you change your perspective, use the FAIL acronym:

- Find a reason: Is there a specific thing that caused this failure? If it was in your control, you know how to change for next time. If it was out of your control, then you can move on to the next letter.
- Accept that it happened: There's no going back in time and no changing the failure. Embracing reality decreases resistance.
- Initiate change: Acknowledging the factors you influenced and what role you played will then require taking accountability to actually make that change.
- Lower your standards: Lower your standards to help you understand that failure is not the worst-case scenario, making it easier to embrace failure in the future.

BREAK IT DOWN

Habits are thought to have three parts: cue, routine, and reward (*Changing Habits*, n.d.). The cue is the trigger that ignites the cycle. The routine is the actual act of the habit. The reward is what is felt after the habit that makes you want to do it again. Consider something like doing dishes. The cue is finishing a meal, the routine is placing the dish in the dishwasher, and the reward is that you have a clean kitchen. This is the best habit to have, but it's not the only habit possible. In an alternate scenario, the cue is finishing a meal, the routine is setting the dirty plate next to the sink, and the reward is not having to do the dishes at the moment. This is a short-term reward, which can result in a huge stack of dishes piling up next to the sink. Despite there being long-term consequences to this option, it can still be easy for our brains to develop this habit since all three parts of the habit are present.

Changing habits requires identifying the cue and routine and then acknowledging the reward. If we focus on habits with long-term rewards rather than short-term rewards, it sets us up for success.

One method of building new habits is the two-minute rule (Clear, n.d.). Any task you want to add to your life can be broken down into the smallest increments possible into tasks that take only a couple of minutes. Do you want to start working out more? Rather than scheduling three hours at the gym on a daily basis, try breaking it down into two-minute tasks. Set timers on your phone to go off throughout the day that remind you to stand up and do some squats or push-ups. This is more realistic to add to your schedule if you struggle with working out rather than expecting yourself to become a full-time gym attendee overnight.

Breaking tasks down into the smallest parts possible makes them easier to tackle and less intimidating and, therefore, more rewarding.

SWAP HANDS

When brushing your teeth in the morning or eating with a utensil, change the hand you're using. This challenges your brain so you're more focused while also forcing your body outside of the habits it's used to.

Many habits become automatic, and the idea of breaking these habits is uncomfortable. When you learn how to embrace the discomfort of change in these small ways, it will then become much easier to sit with that discomfort in bigger ways. Other examples of small habit swapping include:

- tying your shoes using a different knot method (e.g., bunny ears versus a loop)
- sitting in a different spot than you usually do
- taking a different route to work or school

THE LAST-MINUTE LIFESTYLE

Perfectionism can cause us to freeze up, and that can lead to procrastination. When we're dealing with perfectionist tendencies, we tend to have a swarm of overwhelming emotions that can make it hard to focus. Rather than trying to navigate through the murky waters of the ocean of our mind, we decide to swim back to the surface and bury our feet in the sand.

Procrastination is a great escape. It helps us distract ourselves from the challenging feelings and emotions that perfectionism brings on. No one wants to feel like a failure. No one wants to feel like they're not good enough. If you procrastinate by doing something more enjoyable, then you don't have to endure that pain and suffering.

Consider what things you like to procrastinate. I usually become more productive when I'm procrastinating, just not on the thing that requires my attention at the moment. Some people tend to procrastinate with unproductive things, like video games or scrolling social media. These are more obvious signs of procrastination. Ultimately, we know that we should be doing something else, but it's just more enjoyable to watch funny videos or beat your high score.

Productive procrastination is a lot more insidious. It's harder to realize that it is so detrimental because you are making achievements and finding success. For example, if I have to finish a project when working from home, I might end up deciding to reorganize my closet or deep clean the bathroom. These are good things to do, but they aren't pressing issues that require my attention. I still feel like I'm being productive, and I have something to accomplish. I end up fulfilling that goal, and that provides me with immediate relief. Unfortunately, however, I still have to go back to the unfinished work, and all of those feelings I had been avoiding come rushing back. Procrastination is only a temporary relief.

Perfectionism is often thought to be a type of procrastination. The desire to make sure everything is done as best as possible takes a long time. Most of our tasks have a time limit, whether we have to get them done that day or by a certain date in the future. Since perfectionism makes us feel as though nothing is ever good enough, we end up spending a lot more time than we need to get things done.

Some types of procrastinators believe they work better under pressure. The reality is this is likely only because it has become a habit at that point. If you feel as though you like to wait until the day before an assignment is due to get it done, it's simply because that's a method that has worked for you in the past, so your brain stores that information and decides to continue upholding this type of habit.

Procrastination also downplays the eventual consequences because we only have to manage the *idea* of those consequences rather than actually feel them. For example, pushing off a school assignment until the day before it's due feels easy in your mind. You can justify it with a multitude of excuses. If it's Monday and the project is due on Friday, you can tell yourself, *I have four full, long days to get that done. I am just not in the mood today, but I'm sure if I have the right mindset, I'll be more productive tomorrow.*

You also can imagine the worst-case scenario and alleviate yourself from it. You can tell yourself, *Even if I don't start until*

Thursday, I'll still have plenty of time to get it done. It won't take me that long.

Then each day, you end up feeling worse because you weren't productive, so by the time Thursday rolls around, you're having to rush to get through. Nothing feels like it's good enough, and you feel shameful and defeated from an unproductive week. It takes longer than you anticipated because of all of these emotional aspects, and you end up having to submit subpar work.

The last-minute lifestyle ultimately *works,* but it is not as highly successful as it could be. It does not help us feel good about ourselves, and it is not sustainable.

Procrastination is also easy to perpetuate as a perfectionist because, while it does bring undesirable feelings, sometimes those feelings are still easier to endure than the feelings of failure. For example, feeling stressed and rushed to get something done might be less painful than the existential dread of wondering if you're good enough. One is like going to the doctor to get a shot, whereas the other can feel like complex surgery.

Learning how to overcome procrastination is a great step toward reducing perfectionist habits.

SET A TIMER

Invest in a kitchen timer or stopwatch to help you start time chunking, as this can keep you focused. In combination with the small breakdown of tasks mentioned previously, you can then make it easier to time chunk. Time chunking is a way to organize your tasks before you get started in a way that makes them easier to manage. Think of something simple, like cleaning out the fridge. You can chunk tasks into three categories: cleaning, organizing, and deep cleaning. First, you would toss any leftovers and vegetables that have gone bad. Next, you would organize the fridge drawers and door to keep similar foods in the same areas (like putting all the cheese in one drawer and all the sauces in the door). Last, you would deep clean by wiping down the shelves and walls to make it squeaky clean. If you do one thing at a time, it can take longer. If you dump out the leftover rice, wash that container, and then wipe down the shelf it was sitting on, this is going to take longer than chunking the tasks together.

Setting a timer for each of these "chunks" will keep you on track.

One method of time chunking is the Pomodoro Technique. This involves working for 25 minutes and then taking a 5-minute break. You would do this four times, totaling two hours. Next, you would take a longer break, 15-30 minutes, and repeat as needed until you've completed all chunks.

What works best for you will depend on the type of tasks you have to do paired with how long you are able to work. Create your own chunks by timing how long you work before you get distracted. "Distractions" include:

- having a perfectionist thought
- doing something else unrelated to the main task
- getting sidetracked

- feeling the urge to start over or redo something you have already finished

If you notice that you can only work for 15 minutes before one of these distractions starts, then going forward, you know you can chunk tasks into 15-minute sessions, utilizing a timer to keep you on track. Over time, your attention span will increase, as will your ability to lengthen those chunks.

SAY SOMETHING NICE

Positive affirmations can be uncomfortable for some people, but starting with neutrality as the baseline will make it easier to fine-tune your internal monologue. When you notice yourself repeating a negative thought, write it down. Some negative affirmations I've said to myself in the past include:

- I'm the worst.
- This is not good enough.
- Why do I even bother?

These are very damaging to self-esteem. Turning them neutral can help lighten their severity. This would be:

- I'm not the worst.
- I made an effort.
- I know I can try harder.

Once you find a solid neutral ground, it then becomes easier to turn them into positive affirmations. The more you repeat these affirmations to yourself, the more validity they have.

In addition, try adding reassuring statements like "yet" or "but that's okay" to the end of negative affirmations. Examples include:

- I have had no success... yet.
- I have nothing good in my life... yet.
- I'm not very good at my job... but that's okay.
- I have no talents... but that's okay.

While they aren't necessarily positive, they serve as realistic reminders that the negative thoughts you're experiencing are temporary and will pass.

BREATHE, DRINK, AND THINK

Start each day with 15 minutes of breathing exercises, drinking water, and doing nothing but sitting with your thoughts. Often, we wake up and get started with our phone right away, or maybe we rush through morning routines since we're chronically late for work. Scheduling 15-30 minutes of time in the morning to do nothing but breathe and hydrate can be very powerful on the body. You need hydrogen and oxygen to function. Without these vital life sources, you might find yourself feeling lethargic and panicked. A simple breathing exercise to try is to breathe deeply in through your nose and out through your mouth as you count. Try this exercise every day for just three days and you will notice a difference.

Reducing the initial and overpowering emotional state that perfectionist tendencies create is the first stage of overcoming perfectionism once and for all. Once you do this, you will then be able to set more realistic standards for yourself.

CHAPTER 5
GETTING REAL

Perfectionists tend to set themselves up for failure, so setting realistic standards is now needed to ensure success. When will things be good enough? This is a hard thing to judge as a perfectionist since our standards essentially tell us that nothing truly is good enough. It is possible to lower your standards and still take pride in your work, but this is a challenge for perfectionists, as we can often feel like lower standards equal giving up.

A big part of overcoming perfectionism is staying focused on realistic and practical standards rather than letting our minds wander toward the desire for perfection.

I was an aircraft mechanic for more than 20 years until the airline I worked for went out of business due to the reduced travel during the beginning of COVID-19. Often, while working on a job, I would allow myself to become distracted by something minor. I would get so focused on that distraction that I would spend many hours working on it and end up not completing the original task.

One specific instance I can recall is when I was assigned to install the pilot's seat in a cockpit. A pretty standard job for my position, this was something that could easily be completed within a day's work. Honestly, it shouldn't take more than an hour or two at the most. When preparing to install the seat, I noticed a floorboard screw that was not completely tight. I decided to tighten it quickly before installing the seat. I found that the screw was spinning in the hole and would not tighten. While a frustrating discovery, it wasn't something that required immediate attention. I could have written up the loose screw to be fixed later, but instead, I continued working on fixing the screw. It just didn't feel right to continue until everything was perfect.

Unfortunately for me and those waiting for the work to be done, the repair of the screw turned into a sizeable, time-consuming job. When the screw was finally fixed, the workday was over, and I did not get the pilot's seat installed. While the screw was a task that required my attention, it wasn't the initial task I had been given that day, causing me to delay my main priority.

In this instance, and *many* like it, had I stayed focused on my assigned task, I would not have had to tell my boss at the end of the day that I had not gotten my assigned work completed.

For the projects we're tasked with, we often have the main requirements, and these create the basic standards we should reach. Our perfectionist mind sees additional tasks along the way that could be added to our main priorities, and letting those small things go can be incredibly difficult. Knowing how to differentiate between realistic and perfectionist tendencies can help us reduce procrastination and increase focus.

LOWERING STANDARDS

The desire to overcome perfectionism is sometimes formed around how to actually be a *better* perfectionist. Sometimes, we think the act of being a perfectionist is what is actually getting in the way of achieving perfection without realizing that we've set out for impossible standards in the first place. The goal shouldn't lie in knowing how to be *more* perfect— the key to overcoming perfectionist tendencies is knowing how to lower standards and how to be okay with them.

The desire to increase productivity and move on from stress is rooted in our wanting to do better so we can fulfill the fantasy of our perfectionist urges. Unfortunately, this can lead us down the wrong path and away from overcoming these debilitating thoughts. What is really important is maintaining realism and practicality so we can actually achieve any form of success.

This is hard for perfectionists because it's easy to create a system of justification as to why it's important to reach high standards. We tie our ability to be perfect to our self-worth, so it can make it incredibly defeating when we decide to aim lower than our inner desires.

Know that time changes our abilities and perspectives. As a young adult, you wanted to conquer the world, but as you got older, the reality set in that this wasn't possible. Sometimes, lowering our standards can feel like defeat because we had this idealized version of success as a child, teen, and young adult. Now that we aren't fulfilling this long-term fantasy, it feels like we're a failure. However, that youthful mind often discounted reality and overestimated not only our abilities but also the likelihood of achievement based on factors outside of our control.

For example, wanting to be a household name as a celebrity is a great fantasy to strive for as a child. However, when you hit 35 and still haven't landed a role, it might feel defeating to go back to school so you can get a teaching license to become a drama teacher. Realistically, expecting to become famous is like expecting to win the lottery. Being able to work with your craft (like acting) is still incredibly rewarding and something that not everyone is able to do, even if it means teaching rather than becoming famous. Don't compare your adult life to your childhood dreams. It sounds defeating or even depressing, but you don't have to give up on your dreams altogether! What's so bad about choosing one career path instead of the other? Our judgmental voice tells us that the perfect way is the *only* way, and that can be very detrimental to our self-esteem. In addition, you can still audition and explore your craft, but finding a substantial career to help you financially is still important.

There are three levels of standards that can help you determine good standards. Use the MOP acronym:

- Minimum: These are the basic requirements for whatever task or goal you have. This is the bare minimum of what you can achieve to still have "success."
- Optimal: These are standards that are slightly above the minimum while still requiring that you push yourself and stay based on realistic standards.
- Perfect: These are incredibly high standards that often rely on luck, "magic," or unrealistic expectations.

When creating any type of goal, focus on categorizing the potential outcome between these three categories to give you insight and perspective on what is a realistic versus unrealistic standard.

As perfectionists, we often strive for perfection but end up reaching the minimum standards. Optimum goals are what exists in the middle, which is what we should strive for. Learn to strive for optimum because this is the best *possible* based on the resources and abilities we have. Remember that lowering your standards is not the same as giving up (Thibodeaux, n.d.). Giving up is something we're frequently forced to do because we push ourselves far too hard for perfection.

A term that can help you understand how to lower your standards is "excellencism" (Dennis-Tiwary, 2022). This takes all of the beneficial aspects of perfectionism, like striving for high standards, but without the immense expectations, pressure, and anxiety that perfectionists tend to seek. "Perfectionism" makes us feel like we have to reach the top of the ladder, whereas "excellencism" is more focused on how we use our skills and talents to climb the ladder, finding satisfaction wherever we end up because we are able to celebrate the success of the climb. The best way to lower your standards and be *okay* with this is to focus on the process and identify the benefits of failure.

FOCUS ON THE PROCESS

Overcoming perfectionism requires that we overcome the urge to focus on the results. A road trip isn't fun just because of the destination. It's the car games, audiobooks, and long, deep talks with your road trip partner that are the most fun! This is how we have to think of our efforts. When you learn how to be in the moment, you increase your appreciation for the journey.

When focused on results, it increases our state of stress, which takes away our ability to stay present. It then makes trying harder, which can exacerbate perfectionist habits. If you are stressed about a project and you can't stop thinking about failing, then any attempt you make is going to be painful and feel wrong.

With any task, make the process a ritual and more enticing rather than trying to rush through it. If you have to study for an upcoming exam, create a specific playlist of your most inspiring tunes. If you have to clean your apartment before guests visit, make a game out of it with your roommate. If you have to work a long night to catch up with work, make a fancy mocktail and light a candle to make the process more enjoyable.

This way, if failure occurs, you still have an enjoyable memory and don't feel like that time was wasteful. Celebrate small milestones and progress along the way to increase your enjoyment of the process.

IDENTIFY THE BENEFITS OF FAILURE

Embracing failure is more likely to help increase our learning capabilities versus expecting perfection every time. This is because failure forces us to "adapt and change" (Barber, 2021).

Before we start, we hope for success and block out the rest. Challenge yourself to explore the potential benefits that could happen if you were to fail. What could you learn from the process? What would you tell a friend to make them feel better if they were in your shoes and ultimately failed?

Use visualization to go through the motions of some of the worst-case scenarios (while staying realistic). Sure, at any time, a meteor could crash where you are and disrupt the flow of events, but this is unlikely. When I say "realistically speaking," this refers to worst-case scenarios that are most likely to actually occur.

Don't let your superstitious tendencies keep you from visualizing failure. Sometimes, people don't like to think about failure because they believe they'll "jinx" themselves or "manifest" it. This is not the case, and if you are genuinely worried about this, then after you visualize failure, visualize success again so you stay motivated.

It's better to have this perspective on failure and not need it than to need it and not have it.

TIME FLUIDITY

When we're having fun with our closest loved ones, time flies. When we have 30 minutes of work left, those minutes feel like an hour each. This proves that time changes depending on our perspective of it. Newer research has set out to understand the fluidity of time, with some studies showing that time processing occurs in "a large network of neural areas, not just a single brain structure" (Dawson & Sleek, 2018). This goes to show that time perception is an emotional aspect rather than a rigid one.

Parkinson's law is one theory on time that explains how we will use up all the time we are given to complete a task, regardless of how long it actually takes. For example, if you give yourself a day to clean the bathroom even though you could get it done in an hour, you will likely spend the entire day cleaning the bathroom and sometimes even more.

Parkinson's law also theorizes that we open ourselves up to a greater risk of procrastination when we give ourselves too much time (Cherry, 2022). When we give ourselves more time, we then tend to expand our expectations. This is when you will start to find more specific things to add to your to-do list, justifying it by telling yourself things like, *I have plenty of time.*

If we have a lot of time to do something and get it done quickly and efficiently, it can also make us feel as though we didn't try hard enough. We might grow concerned, wondering if we forgot something or overanalyzing why it was "too easy."

Just like you should find your middle ground for standards —the "optimum" level—find your middle time ground. If something takes you an average of 30 minutes to complete, don't only give yourself 30 minutes. Instead, give yourself around 45 minutes. An hour might be too much.

ANALYZE YOUR SCHEDULE

Scheduling is an important way to create a realistic time map for how we'll spend our day. As a perfectionist, we often stuff it with as many tasks as we can think of rather than focusing on as many tasks that are actually possible. Routines are important for keeping us on track but, like our standards, they must be realistic.

Evaluate your schedule to see if it's something realistic you're capable of or if you're simply creating a schedule you hope to use. When looking at your schedule, it should be something that's exciting for you and feels realistic. If you look at your schedule and think to yourself, *How will I ever get all of this done?* then it's likely overstuffed.

Ensure you don't schedule yourself down to the minute, either. For an example of a morning routine, an unrealistic schedule might be:

- 6 a.m.: wake up
- 6:05 a.m.: brush teeth

- 6:10 a.m.: go for a jog
- 6:30 a.m.: shower
- 6:40 a.m.: get dressed
- 6:45 a.m.: eat breakfast
- 7 a.m.: read
- 7:30 a.m.: journal
- 8 a.m.: do the dishes
- 8:15 a.m.: pack lunch
- 8:30 a.m.: leave for work

As you can see, this morning routine is great because it has exercising, journaling, reading, and some cleaning. However, it is incredibly strict and can be overwhelming to view. If it ends up taking five more minutes to go for a jog or do the dishes, it can throw the rest of the routine off, causing more stress.

A more realistic schedule might look something like this:

- 6-7 a.m.: exercise and get ready
- 7-8 a.m.: eat breakfast and either read or journal
- 8-9 a.m.: pack lunch and get ready to leave for work

As you can see, this is a nice and easy time chunk. If there is time to do both reading and journaling, that's great, but staying focused on just one can help free up some time and add variety to the schedule. Something like doing light dishes from eating breakfast or prepping lunch can be a part of the last hour before heading to work. Keeping some fluidity and allowing for delays will decrease rigidity and decrease stress.

EMBRACE SINGLE-TASKING

Multitasking can be more time-consuming than doing one thing at a time. Learning how to avoid multitasking and adding more time to allocate to tasks can make them more realistically achievable. Research shows that multitasking makes us more distracted and decreases focus, even in times when we are single-tasking (Cherry, 2023).

Switching back and forth between tasks takes more energy because your mind has to switch on and off.

Single-tasking allows us to reach autopilot. When we stay focused on a single task, we have the ability to streamline the process by reducing our focus and letting our mind and body go with the motion. This automation makes things faster, whereas swapping between states of two tasks prevents us from reaching that automation.

When you switch back and forth, you might be more likely to check the clock as well, which can start thoughts of second-guessing yourself by thinking things like, *I'm not doing this fast enough* or *I'm wasting too much time.*

Some tasks can be multi-tasked, like working out while listening to music or folding laundry while watching a movie. The key here is that one of the tasks is more passive (like music or watching TV), and the other is more active and mostly requires your body rather than your mind.

SOCIAL STANDARDS

It's easy for us to set impossible standards for ourselves because we are the ones attempting to make the commitment to achieving this. Would you ever ask someone else to meet the standards that you're asking? Chances are, likely not.

This proves that deep down, you know you are setting standards that are way too hard to reach. On top of this, acknowledging that it's too much to ask also acknowledges that if these standards aren't reached, everything will be okay. The severity isn't placed on making sure the goals are reached; instead, there's immense pressure because *you* want to be the one to make these achievements. The idea of being perfect feels great, so the idea that we *could* reach these standards still provides a morsel of relief, which is why we often strive so hard to reach these goals.

Look in your social group or at the employees at your job. When setting a goal, ask yourself if you'd set the same goal for others or if you think it would be too much to ask. If it's too much, there's a good chance you're still setting yourself up for failure. Remember to focus on optimum goals, not perfect goals.

CHAPTER 6
PRIORITIZING YOU

Putting everyone else first is common for us perfectionists, but that then creates normalcy around prioritizing ourselves last.

Perfectionists tend to be people pleasers. Combine that with negative self-talk, and you have a recipe for disaster in terms of self-care. Identifying your energy sources, focusing on yourself, and learning the skill of saying no to others will help ensure you stay focused on your needs.

I've always struggled to say no because I want to help people out. I like genuinely seeing them happy, and I pride myself on being a friend others can turn to when they need help. However, much like many things in life, I've taken this desire too far and have neglected my own needs in the process. Over the years, I've learned that people will still like me even if I'm not perfect. Failing to realize this in the past led me to become resentful of others after feeling unappreciated. This also caused me to struggle with feeling burnt out, exacerbating my already struggling self-care routine.

When thinking of self-care, you might get the image of someone relaxing in a spa, receiving facials and massages. While this is a form of self-care, basic self-care is based on our human needs. If you were to care for a puppy or even a child, you'd make sure they were fed, bathed, and had a place to get adequate sleep. You'd check in with how they were developing to ensure they were learning and growing in the best way possible. This care must be done on ourselves, *by* ourselves, to ensure we have all of our needs met. The perfectionist mind is a busy one that can convince itself these types of things don't matter so as to prioritize other, seemingly more important, tasks. However, failing to provide yourself with adequate self-care will only make the stress and anxiety of being a perfectionist that much worse.

ENERGIZING YOURSELF

What we fuel our body with and how we spend our energy will be very impactful on how we mentally and physically feel. This is also a very important part of self-care on an emotional and physical level. Our bodies are machines and can only work as well as what we provide them with. If you are not providing adequate nutrition, you will be left feeling lethargic and anxious.

I'm not going to tell you that there is a right way or a wrong way to eat. Any form of eating can be "healthy" eating. I don't want to perpetuate disordered eating or cast shame onto anyone's lifestyle. However, as a perfectionist, it's essential to note the way that our nourishment has a biological impact on the way we feel. Certain anxiety-inducing foods can lead to higher stress levels. For example, I've found that simply replacing black coffee with green tea is a great way to reduce caffeine levels. When I used to drink strong black coffee multiple times a day, I would find my heart racing and feel shaky overall. This would only make my perfectionist tendencies worse.

In addition, it's important to note that the all-or-nothing thinking that perfectionists tend to perpetuate will impact one's ability to stay consistent with a nutritious diet. Sometimes, there's an idea that you have to have a perfect diet or not even bother trying, which can lead to restriction or binging. You need 21 meals a week. Eleven healthy meals and 10 less-than-nutritious meals are much better than giving up altogether and ignoring your nutrition.

Obsessive thoughts of perfectionists can seep into our body image, having detrimental effects on how we view our relationship with food. Food is also very rewarding, so alternatively, it can be used as a punishment or weapon against us. Have you ever held off eating lunch, only allowing yourself to do so after you finish work? Have you ever skipped breakfast in favor of getting more work done? Food is a *requirement*, not a luxury, and it's important for our perfectionist minds to grasp this concept.

In addition, water is incredibly hydrating, and poor hydration can even mimic symptoms of anxiety. You need around six to eight glasses of plain water a day (Naidoo, 2020). Drink water with every meal, even if you have another beverage, and especially if that beverage is alcoholic or caffeinated, as these are all diuretics that reduce hydration intake.

GET BETTER SLEEP

Most of us know it's important to eat right and exercise (even if we don't do it well). However, sleep is often neglected, but sometimes stress can arise simply from feeling overly tired.

Perfectionism is often experienced and perpetuated in the mind. However, troubleshooting the ways that we neglect our health can reduce symptoms of stress and anxiety, making it easier to manage our emotions.

This starts by identifying what you do leading up to the moments when you go to bed, how you sleep throughout the night, and then what happens after you wake up.

For starters, ensure that you maintain a similar routine every night. You don't have to schedule your sleep and wake time down to the minute; however, you should be falling asleep within the same 30-minute range and waking up within that same range every day of the week. This helps create a consistent regulation through all of your bodily systems, from the cardiovascular system to your hormonal system. Ensure when you go to bed that you give yourself 20 to 30 minutes to cool down before you fall asleep. If you lay in bed and scroll through social media on your phone, you're likely exposed to advertisements, loud and colorful images, and sometimes even stressful news or videos. This gets your mind worked up, and all that energy carries with you throughout the night.

This will start your morning off with a more stressful mind and body. Pick something more relaxing, whether it's watching a peaceful show if you prefer TV or reading or journaling. Meditating is also a great thing to do before bed.

Ensure that there are no lights or noises that keep you alert or distracted throughout the night. Even something as small as a night-light can disturb your sleep. If you do need to sleep with some form of light on, consider using a timer so it shuts off after you fall asleep. In the morning, ensure that you give yourself optimal time to wake up. The mind needs to adjust after sleeping for that long period. Stepping outside, feeling the fresh air, and seeing the sun can help your mind realize that it's time to wake up, making this transition period easier. In addition, remember to hydrate as you wake up, especially since coffee and caffeinated drinks are diuretics, as mentioned previously.

SIT WITH NATURE

Nature is chaotic, so getting out and exploring our beautiful Mother Earth can help us take good care of ourselves while appreciating the beauty of uncertainties.

Sitting in and with nature connects you back to your natural roots. There are four corners to health. This includes our nutrition, which encapsulates food and hydration. The second is sleep and rest. The third is your mental state and stress levels. Last, exercise is an important part of your health.

All of our bodies need a certain amount of physical movement. One of the best ways to do this is to get out in nature. Start by going for more nature walks. This is a great form of multitasking because you're getting healthy movement for your body while also experiencing some of the beauty of nature. Not all of us live next to a conservatory or a national park, so you might not have access to a ton of nature. However, even simply walking through a small patch of grass can be enough to help connect you back to soil and greenery. If you are somebody who prefers home workouts, then add nature to your workout space. Invest in some plants to fill your guest bedroom, where you can practice yoga and other forms of healthy stretching. Additionally, just sitting in nature is also important. Stick your feet in the grass or the sand and deeply breathe in all of the senses of nature.

PROTECTING YOUR PEACE

Setting boundaries is an important part of maintaining our management over perfectionism. Boundaries aren't to be confused with rules. For example, most areas have the rule that littering is illegal and could result in a fine. Most of us have a boundary with ourselves to not litter—not because we want to avoid getting in trouble, but because we know how detrimental it can be to the environment.

Boundaries are crucial to set in regard to how you spend your time and to whom you choose to give it. Boundaries are also important to set with yourself so you stay within the range of realistically achievable tasks. The urge to say yes to everyone as a perfectionist is common because having to say no makes us worry that we might let others down. Will they see we are imperfect? Will they reject us or become upset? Saying no and turning things down taps into our deep fear of not being able to accomplish all of the standards we set for ourselves.

Saying no is uncomfortable at first, but it is an important practice to help you maintain your peace, sanity, and self-image. By acknowledging the importance of saying no and keeping time to yourself, you recognize that you are a human deserving of the things that you truly desire.

CHANGE YOUR SPACE

Finding a small way to change up your space can make it easier to shift into a new mindset while also doing something nice for yourself. This is also essential so you have a safe space you can call your own. We all deserve to have moments to ourselves, and having an inviting and warm space to do so will help you foster a healthier relationship with yourself. Consider both small and large changes to create a new space to help your mind snap into new territory as well. Examples of changes include:

- rearrange furniture
- declutter and invest in a shelf or organizational cubes for easier storage
- paint a wall with a brighter coat or add an inspiring mural

- change a normal light bulb with a color-changing one
- invest in a throw pillow or new blanket to help spruce up a couch or bed without having to buy all-new furniture

FIVE DIFFERENT WAYS

Identify five different ways to say no to different scenarios that are likely to come up. Having small scripts ready and practicing them on your own makes it easier to say no when the time comes. In addition, remember that you can always ask for more time. Not every response has to be a yes or a no.

Think of five situations in the past in which you should've said no, but instead, you said yes. Write these down and create a small script for each so if they come up again, you know what to say. For example from my own experience: A friend asked me to help them move out of their fourth-floor apartment. I should've said no because I had only recently recovered from a sprained ankle. I said yes and helped them but ended up having to take a couple of days off work to recover my sore ankle once again. What I should have said was, "I wish I could, but I recently sprained my ankle and won't be able to!"

This is a simple way of saying no. You can also offer an alternative. For example, I could have offered to pet sit their dogs while they moved so they didn't have to worry about them. At the end of the day, always remind yourself that "no" is a complete sentence.

FIND YOUR CHAOS

As perfectionists, it can sometimes feel as though we rely on chaotic things like procrastination. We get so used to the stress that we unconsciously seek it out, sometimes through self-destructive behavior. Finding something to help you experience that chaoticness can free your mindset to overcome some of the high standards and barriers that you created. Some examples of chaotic things include:

- experimental music
- horror movies or art films
- extreme sports, like rock climbing or sky diving

What is something that is both slightly uncomfortable and exhilarating? Anything that scares you might be something to seek out and try! Once you find your chaos, you then create an outlet to experience some of the stress that your body naturally craves without damaging your professional, personal, and financial life.

CHAPTER 7
EXPOSURE TO
IMPERFECTION

F eedback and criticism are hard to take. They are both great ways to help us grow and improve, especially in areas we are passionate about. But if we are taking that criticism through a perfectionist lens, it can tap into some of those insecurities rather than hearing the value of the advice and wanting to make a change.

In the perfectionist mind, we struggle with fear over the worst-case scenario. Often, this scenario is rooted in our failure. As we build up the intensity of failure in our minds, it makes it scarier to have to confront it. However, most failure is not that big of a deal. If we learn how to overcome that intense fear, it becomes easier to keep working on the tasks at hand to push past the fear. If one small form of criticism arises, it can then sometimes validate all of the other fears you have about yourself.

For example, if you are working on an art project like a painting, you might keep going over and over the canvas, desperately trying to get it "just right." You feel insecure with your work and, therefore, yourself. You question your abilities, and your thoughts spiral, leaving you questioning yourself in general. Then, when it comes time to show off your painting, someone points out a small mistake. That tiny form of criticism then validates all of the other thoughts you had about yourself as well. You think to yourself, *They saw the imperfections in my painting, so everyone must also see the imperfections in my life.* This is why submitting work can be so hard—there's the potential that every fear we have about ourselves will be proven to be true.

The only way to get through this intense fear is through exposure therapy and by acknowledging the things that are in and out of our control.

GET REJECTED

Having small acts of rejection can make the real deal a lot less scary. These include small moments where we get turned down, criticized, or endure failure. This will help us understand that these moments of rejection are not nearly as scary as we thought they might be. Start small with little forms of rejection therapy. This means simply putting yourself out there in social situations.

Walk up to somebody and ask them what time it is. Most of us have our cell phones or a watch, so we don't really need to ask strangers what time it is. However, this is a way to get used to asking people questions with the chance that they might turn you down. Somebody might say, "I don't know" or "I don't have my phone on me." You can simply walk away after and realize that hearing "no" from somebody else isn't as bad as it seems.

Call up a local grocery store or a restaurant and ask them something silly, like, "Do you have any free food for me?" You can also hide your phone number if you are really worried about the small moments of rejection. You can also try these moments of rejection in small personal settings with people you feel safe around. For example, ask a friend if they'll come over and do your dishes. They might laugh and ask if you're joking, or maybe they'll actually do it, saving you a chore!

Then, take an even bigger step and start to put yourself in situations that you actually care about. This means asking that person out whom you've had a crush on for years. It means applying for a job that seems like it might be a little bit outside of your capabilities. This could mean applying for a scholarship or a specific schooling program. Once you start with a small rejection, you can build your way up to the more serious forms of rejection.

CIRCLE OF CONTROL

Knowing what is in and out of your control can make it much easier to know where to focus your energy so you can let go of the things that don't need as much of your attention. There are only a few things we have control over in this life. Most of us understand that we can't control things like the weather or even our health. We can't control whether or not it's going to rain or snow or if there's going to be a tornado. We can try to eat right and get enough physical movement to prevent certain illnesses, but at the end of the day, certain cancers and diseases are not biased toward somebody's level of general health. Genetic conditions could creep up at any moment.

Another huge factor we need to embrace that is outside of our control is other people. You can't control somebody else's actions, thoughts, or emotions. You can't control what they say or how they choose to interpret information. You can't even control their perception of you. Sometimes, we like to feel as though we have control over this by changing our appearance or catering our behavior so we only act a certain way around specific individuals. At the end of the day, you can't ever understand what is completely going on in somebody's mind; therefore, it is impossible to have any form of control over them.

The only type of control we have is over our own thoughts and actions. We control how we respond to our emotions. You can't always help it if somebody makes you agitated or angry, but it is entirely within your control whether or not that's a fleeting feeling or something that is going to impact your day-to-day life. You can't always control certain decisions that are made about your life or what happens in the future, but you can control how you respond to them. For example, you can't control whether or not you get a job; however, you can control whether or not you use this as a reason to give up altogether or to simply refine your resume and try again.

Our attitude is completely within our control, and recognizing what's inside our circle of control and what is outside our circle of control can help free up some of our energy. When you are constantly putting energy into trying to change the things that are outside of your control, you are left feeling exhausted, burnt out, and disappointed.

In your journal, draw a circle. Inside the circle, write the things in your control, such as:

- your emotions
- your opinions
- your beliefs

Fill out the rest of the circle with your own ideas. Outside of the circle, write down everything that is outside of your control, like:

- the weather
- your genetics
- other's opinions

Seeing a visual representation of this circle can make it easier for you to comprehend what truths you might've been resisting. After that, take a moment to reflect on some of the things you've been trying to control that have been causing additional stress and anxiety. Then, consider what things within your circle you've been avoiding taking responsibility for.

EMBRACING PAST MISTAKES

Perfectionists are detail-oriented, which means it's easy to understand and identify the complexities and nuances of any situation. This is great for thorough work but not so great when it comes to internal rumination. Often, we are left thinking of the past, seeing all of the small, detailed ways we could've made changes.

If you are like me, you struggle with regret over the past. As we get older, we have even more time and experience we can look back on and evaluate through a perfectionist lens. Often, regret can be confused with mourning (Sawhney, 2021). In a way, regret is mourning because it's easy to feel a sense of loss over the life you thought you were going to have. When you reach your adult years, you start to realize the things you wished for as a child and teen aren't as they seem. These realizations are sometimes painful and often uncomfortable. In trying to control that discomfort, we start to blame ourselves internally, disregarding the factors that were outside of our control. We tend to focus on the idea that things would have been better if only we had done this or that without realizing that there is a good chance that things could've even been worse!

I have a friend who, luckily, escaped an emotionally toxic relationship. She often talks about how regretful she is that she endured this for so long. They had started dating in their early 20s and didn't break up until their mid-30s. She often discusses regrets and wishes she had never committed herself to this person. She wonders how much better life would've been had she met someone else or been able to explore dating in her younger years.

What I've started to remind her is that things could have just as easily happened in a different way. She could've found someone else who was even more manipulative and verbally abusive. She could've dated multiple people who stole from her, cheated on her, and treated her poorly. She also could've stayed in that relationship for an even longer period in her life. While it's not easy to get over regrets, the key is to remind ourselves of the balance of reality. Sure, life could've been better, but it also could've been much, much worse.

When we get stuck on regrets, there's this assumption that if we hadn't done what we did, things would've magically been better. It's easy to say that now, but there's no way of knowing how things could've turned out.

Learning how to look back on past mistakes and reevaluate them can make it easier to embrace some of our biggest regrets. To do this:

1. Identify some past mistakes or regrets in terms of situations that you had control/influence over.
2. Notice the way they changed life's trajectory and label ways that things could have gone worse.
3. Identify something good that's come from it, even if it was just a hard life lesson to learn.
4. Sit with gratitude that these mistakes have happened the way they did rather than turning out worse than you could've imagined. In addition, you can also show gratitude for your ability to healthily

reflect and find substantial reasoning for what went on.

Going forward, stay balanced when experiencing regret and build hope that these mistakes will still mean something in the future. Embrace the idea that even when things aren't perfect, life is leading you down the right path.

SHARE YOUR FAILURE

It can feel good to share our successes because we get praise from other people. Sharing your failures can also provide you with a sense of reassurance and validation from others.

For this activity, talk about a failure you had with a close relative or friend next time you're chatting. You'll likely find that they tell you it's okay and provide reminders that you are human.

After, consider if this person had made the same mistake. Would you judge them? Would you be hard on them? Would you make them feel bad about themselves? Chances are, you'd reassure them with open arms, so it's essential we do the same for ourselves.

DO SOMETHING YOU DON'T LIKE

What's something you really loathe? What is something that makes you uncomfortable that you don't enjoy?

What you might find is that you dislike this because you aren't perfect at it, don't know everything there is to know about it, or you are afraid of being judged by associating yourself with it. When we aren't perfect at certain things, it's easy to ignore them. The perfectionist mind wants to be the best but often disregards growth and challenges that are required to get there.

Step outside of your comfort zone and try something you dislike as a way to force self-reflection and experience some perfectionist discomfort. Pick something you're bad at. For example, I was never a super athletic person. I was often picked last in gym class and failed to do pull-ups and push-ups when we were all tested for these exercises. I purchased a pull-up bar for my office doorway and started trying to do one a day. It took me about two weeks before I was able to comfortably do a single pull-up, but the joy I felt was exhilarating. It's easy to choose things that we are good at to boost our self-esteem, but true empowerment arises when we set out to reach a challenge and are able to overcome the obstacles it takes to get there.

FORGIVE AND THANK YOURSELF

Forgiving yourself for past mistakes is important and requires that you experience that discomfort again.

Forgiveness requires that the mistake-maker takes accountability. Without excessive self-blame, how can you take responsibility for your past mistakes? Admitting your wrongs is uncomfortable, especially because it requires you to let go of excuses.

Next, actually say, "I'm sorry." Ensure that this is followed by "for..." An apology is meaningless if the person apologizing doesn't acknowledge the actual wrongdoing.

Then, you have to forgive yourself. Show empathy. There's a reason you made the mistake. State this out loud and label what motivated you to make this decision.

Take it a step further and thank yourself for these mistakes or thank yourself for getting away from them or moving past them. In the example mentioned previously about my friend in the regretful relationship, she might tell herself, "I'm sorry for staying in the relationship for longer than I should have, even though I knew it wasn't good for me. I was afraid of leaving and didn't know what else to do. I am grateful that I finally got the strength to leave once and for all."

While it's not easy, it can lift a heavy burden off your chest and mind so you can continue to move forward in your healing journey.

CHAPTER 8
GETTING THROUGH THE MOMENT

L earning how to embrace the moment will help you get used to pulling yourself from the sticky trap of perfectionism.

For most of my life, I was focused on the next moment. I was always thinking of the future steps that would be happening before I was even finished with the one that I was currently working on. I was always worried about what new anxieties might present themselves in my life, and I was constantly rehearsing conversations in my head that would never happen. I would prepare for the worst and always focus on creating backup plans, even though most of the situations would ultimately turn out in my favor. It wasn't until I started working through my perfectionism that I realized just how much time had been wasted due to this excessive stress and anxiety.

I couldn't remember some of the good times that my friends and family would talk about fondly. Instead, I would find myself triggered back to that moment and think about how anxious I was. This happened even with memories involving good times, like vacations. I would be nervous about making sure that everything went perfectly and that all the travels were completed efficiently. At the time, I thought that perfect planning was essential for ensuring I had a good time. What I failed to realize was just how much I lost due to my constant state of panic.

The perfectionist mind is always on the go. It's always trying to plan for every little step. This depletes all of the good things that can come from living in the moment.

THIS MINDFULNESS MOMENT

Mindfulness is a powerful tool to overcome perfectionist tendencies. Perfectionists are often caught up in the future or ruminating over the past, so utilizing a mindfulness or meditation practice can help confront unhelpful thoughts (Garone, 2021).

The act of mindfulness provides us with a moment to stop and think about whether what we are feeling is true or if it is only fueling and perpetuating these impossible idealistic standards. We are all living in the moment in that we are breathing and circulating blood. We are conscious, but we aren't always aware.

Mindfulness is a dedication and practice set out to help you embrace the moment. Even when you are feeling sick, stressed, and tired, you can raise bodily, spatial, and emotional awareness over the present.

As we increase mindfulness, we can increase emotional presence, making it easier to be empathetic to others and strengthening our awareness. For example, how many times has someone stood far too close to you in line at the grocery store checkout? Did you ever struggle to get past someone who stopped in the middle of a walkway? Have you ever lived with a roommate who was constantly leaving their messes around for someone else to deal with? These are all small ways that we lack awareness of the present. Externally, this lack of awareness impacts those who are left picking up the messes or rerouting their path. Internally, however, awareness impacts the individual the most, as they are lost in a moment other than the present.

This practice gets us through temporarily as our minds accept what is happening around us. Mindfulness also makes it easier to reduce self-criticism for more neutral thoughts. Perfectionism thrives off of the urge to make ourselves better, so we are constantly seeking improvement. Learning to utilize a mindfulness-based activity in your daily life will help you learn how to accept yourself for who you are.

ICE THERAPY

While there isn't a ton of research on cold therapy, studies have shown that regular use of icy water, like cold showers, can help reduce symptoms of depression (Cherney, 2020).

Ice therapy is a practical way for you to help reduce your anxiety and snap you into the moment. When you wake up in the morning of the winter months and you have to get out from under the warm blankets, you're likely jolted awake. When you step outside and have to sit in your ice-cold car as the heater warms up, you are likely very focused and present. The cold alerts our senses, so we have to focus on the moment. It creates a sense of urgency and encourages awareness. Have you ever jumped into an icy cold pool? This shocks your system in a way similar to getting burned.

If you touch a hot pan or sip a hot cup of coffee, your body suddenly becomes snapped into the moment and puts all of your attention on this hot object. You have to pull away from it very quickly to help prevent further hurt. The thing about cold therapy is that it's not as damaging as touching something hot, so you can elicit that same jolt without causing permanent damage.

Cold therapy is a safe way for you to utilize some of those natural survival tactics to pull you into the moment. On the smallest level, start by grabbing an ice cube from your freezer and holding it in your hand. Watch as it melts away. Focus on the sensations that are happening. Of course, if you experience any serious physical pain, put the ice cube in the sink to finish melting so you don't hurt yourself.

Take it a step further and try using an ice bowl. This involves filling up a bowl with the coldest water possible. Then, fill the bowl with ice cubes. You can also fill a pitcher with water and keep it in the fridge to help speed up the process and make the water colder. You can even use ice packs instead of ice cubes to prevent wasting water (just ensure that it's safe to use on your skin.) Then, dunk your face into the ice bath for at least two seconds. Most importantly, be careful not to gasp from the shock while your face is underwater!

Build your way up to 10 seconds. This can help snap your focus and pull all of your senses to the moment. Last, try an ice bath or an ice-cold shower. An ice bath is essentially the same thing as the ice bowl, just using your bathtub and dunking your entire body into the bath rather than only your face. Additionally, an ice-cold shower is a great way to wake up in the morning and get your mind started on a particularly stressful day. It's hard to think about all of your regrets and fears over the future when you're trying to focus on staying warm in the moment.

MINDFUL EATING

Eating is such a passive activity that it can easily become mindless when we're not paying attention. When was the last time you ate while watching TV or even in your car on the way to work? The lack of awareness when eating can lead us to overeat and also lose enjoyment from the process in general.

Perfectionists often have disordered eating habits, so mindful eating is a helpful practice to make awareness a more regular part of your life. Since eating is something that you have to do multiple times a day, you can create normalcy around mindfulness through this activity.

To practice, pick your favorite fruit or vegetable. Sit at the kitchen or dining room table without any noises, electronics, or other distractions present. Take your first small bite, let it sit in your mouth for a moment, and notice the flavors and textures. Slowly take one bite and chew it as many times as possible before swallowing. Before taking your next bite, sit with this feeling for a moment. How does it feel in your body? What thoughts are passing through your mind? Not all meals have to be eaten in this slow of a process, but starting with something small, like a simple apple or carrot, can help you reevaluate some of the thoughts you have when eating.

To take it to the next level, cook a classic meal from scratch and then mindfully enjoy it, savoring every moment. Pick a meal to make from homemade, whole foods. This means foods that are not premixed or a blend of multiple ingredients. For example, if you're going to make spaghetti, salsa, or a salad, you would use homemade pasta sauce, fresh pico de gallo, and hand-mixed dressing rather than store-bought jars and bottles. Watching the process of a meal transform from a simple tomato into a delectable dish can increase your mindfulness over what really goes into a meal.

FOCUS THROUGH SENSORY IMMERSION

Perfectionism causes us to get caught in a mental loop. This all happens in our brains, so connecting back to our body's senses will make it easier to focus on the present and overcome paralyzing thoughts.

You have five senses:

- sight
- touch

- sound
- smell
- taste

To increase mindfulness, focus on incorporating sensory activities into your routine that activate all of these. For example, when baking, you see the exact measurements you have to use, you feel the flour and dough in your hands, you hear the mixer blend ingredients, and your smell and taste are intensely activated as you enjoy the entire process. Other activities that use all of your senses include gardening, working with clay or other artistic mediums, repurposing old furniture, or reading books in the library. The only sense some of these don't use is your taste. However, you can smell the soil, wood stains, and old paper pages of the books. You can see, hear, and feel a multitude of senses when working with these activities. They also help to keep you physically grounded in the moment because they require your focus. When participating in these types of activities, identify one thing that can be associated with each of your five senses. You might also consider chewing a specific flavor of gum or sucking on a certain type of candy while doing these things to help ensure your focus is pulled while participating.

Even when you are not doing much at all, you can increase mindfulness by identifying one thing to associate with each of your five senses. When riding the subway to work, you hear the train move along the tracks, you see the passengers looking at their phones, you feel the seat under your body, you smell the mints from the passenger next to you, and you can taste the coffee from your travel mug.

In addition to sensory activities, try some of the following exercises to help you increase focus and awareness to help reduce anxious thoughts:

BUG-WATCHING

Bird-watching is a popular activity for those who enjoy nature. Another creature just as fascinating is the insect. Much like all animals, they are fascinating creatures with interesting lifestyles. There are many creatures all around us, and looking at the little things can help you utilize your detail-oriented skills in a more neutral and less judgmental way.

Find an outdoor area where you feel safe and can sit for at least 15 minutes. Take a moment to bring awareness to the present. Now, look around until you find a bug. Lift a rock or look under structures for spiders if you're struggling to find one. Alternatively, drop a couple of crumbs on the ground and come back a few minutes later to see if any ants have appeared.

Next, simply watch its activities, what it does, and where it goes. You don't have to do anything other than observe the moment and sit with your thoughts. This is a small and simple way to bring more mindfulness to the present.

MINDFULNESS JAR

Each time you experience perfectionist tendencies, fill a jar with a small item, like stones, shells, beads, or even coins.

Keep it in an area where you work, like your home office. These moments of perfectionist tendencies include:

- making harsh judgments against yourself
- getting stuck in the fear of the future
- ruminating on past regrets or mistakes
- fixing things that don't really need to be fixed (at least at the moment)
- making assumptions about your self-worth

Make a list of additional perfectionist tendencies that you notice to help you have a set of rules to follow, and add more as you become aware of them. Tell a friend, roommate, or spouse so they can call out these moments even when you aren't aware of what you're doing. This will help build a visual representation of perfectionism so you can bring mindfulness back into the moment when your thoughts are spiraling. I found that I filled my jar with coins after a few days. I had to switch to stones since I didn't have enough change on me to keep up! Once you realize just how frequently you perpetuate these habits, you can then increase the power you have over changing these thoughts.

BLIND TASTE TEST

Another activity to help increase mindfulness around eating or tasting is to do a blind taste test.

Purchase three different brands of your favorite beverage, even if it's bottled water. Next, find three of the same style cups and use a small sticker or piece of tape to label them from one to three on the bottom so you can't see the stickers.

Put one in each glass, then mix the glasses up so you don't know which glass contains which drink. Savor each sip of all three to try and determine which is which. This forces you to be very mindful of flavors or textures. Alternatively, try switching up the type of container the beverage is in. For example, if you choose a cola, you can use a can, a glass bottle, and a plastic bottle as your three beverages. The differences are small and might be hard to notice at all, but the process will still help you increase your mindfulness skills.

CHAPTER 9
PUTTING YOURSELF BACK OUT THERE

W e don't just want to be perfect, but we also want to be perceived as perfect, and that puts excessive stress on our social life. In fact, studies show that perfectionists are more likely to struggle with social anxiety and stress in general (Chen, 2022).

Perfectionists can be withdrawn and isolated because of their fear of judgment. When you struggle to have people in your life who lift your spirits, it contributes to negative perspectives that you aren't good enough or undeserving of love.

Social anxiety can be hard to understand because it's not that we are afraid of other people, but instead, we have a "fear of being negatively evaluated by others in social situations" (Etherson, 2021).

This added anxiety can make it even harder to interact because we already feel overwhelmed with the stress of what to say. Social interaction can be challenging for anyone, but for the perfectionist, there are additional standards to meet on top of the basic nervousness of socialization.

As a perfectionist, you likely struggle with the idea that everything that leaves your mouth has to be perfect. You want to be funny and intelligent, and at times, you might even have the urge to boast about yourself to prove that you are worthy and you fit in with social groups. This can leave us searching our brains for points of internal value so as to have evidence to share with others. Not only does this distract us in the moment, but if we can't think of anything to come up with, we're left feeling defeated and with low self-esteem.

There's also pressure to live our lives in a certain way so as to come off as more professional, appealing, or interesting to other people. Our fear of judgment isn't just something experienced when around others but can also impact us when we are alone. Have you ever wanted to watch a specific movie, eat a certain food, or try a certain activity only to end up not doing it because you were afraid of judgment? Even in times when we are by ourselves, we can hear the judgment and voices of others seep into our minds, making it difficult to live the lives we want.

JUST AS AFRAID AS YOU

There's a common saying that reassures those afraid of spiders or other insects: They're just as afraid of you as you are of them. This is something we can apply to our view of others when fearing socialization. It's not that others are afraid of us, but they are at least likely struggling with their own anxieties, just as you are.

In addition, you're more likely to notice your flaws than other people are. We know the shape of our nose and mouth and every bump, freckle, or scar across our bodies. We pay attention when it looks like we've added a few pounds to our waistline or when new gray hairs and wrinkles appear. Others tend to notice these only if they are significant changes (like your entire head of hair turning gray) and if they haven't seen you in a while. They are far less likely to notice little flaws here and there.

The thing is, we also skew these perceptions of ourselves, so we hyper-fixate on certain parts and disregard others. There are even some theories that we wouldn't be able to recognize ourselves or our doppelgangers if we saw them out in public, as we have such a skewed perception of our faces (Gorvett, 2016).

As perfectionists, we have the tendency to reduce the flaws of others, make unfair comparisons, and disregard the deficiencies of other people (Chand, 2020). We then increase our own flaws and focus on our worst qualities, which leaves us never feeling good enough.

Other people are likely to see the uniqueness or beauty you have versus fixating on the flaws. In fact, some research suggests that we are up to 20% more attractive than how we might perceive ourselves (*The Math Behind Beauty*, 2008).

In addition, others are more empathetic than we think. Even if they do notice your flaws, they aren't sitting there thinking,

"Yikes, they are not attractive." They simply notice it and move on. Anyone who *does* think this way isn't worth our time or effort.

Sometimes, judgment is just the first reaction others have, so if they say something hurtful, remember that they might be suffering more from the regret they feel after saying it or they didn't mean it to come out as judgmental as it seemed. If someone tells you, "You look tired," it might sting. Is it the bags under your eyes? Is it the pronounced wrinkles or dry skin? Is it disheveled hair or clothing? You might panic, wondering what they meant. Perhaps they are just referring to the look in your eyes or the tone of your voice. While it might be a hurtful thing that doesn't need to be said, it's essential to not assume the worst intention from other people's comments. To help you begin to reduce the negative side effects of perfectionist-induced social anxiety, it's important to utilize visualization and positive self-talk.

TALK TO YOURSELF

The image of talking to yourself tends to be synonymous with mental instability, but in reality, it's very helpful in getting comfortable with yourself. It also has health benefits, like increasing motivation, focus, and critical thinking skills (*Talking to Yourself*, 2022).

Start with something as small as smiling at yourself in the mirror. You might feel a little crazy the first time—I know I did. But don't worry; the more you practice, the more comfortable it will feel. Smiling helps reduce heart rate and triggers your brain to release stress-fighting molecules (*The Health Benefits of Smiling*, n.d.).

Afterward, take it a step further by saying reassuring and positive things to yourself in the mirror. Before a big day at work or an anxiety-inducing social event, look in the mirror and say things like:

- I've got this.
- I'm all good.
- Everything is going to be okay.

Seeing yourself say these reassuring things with a smile will decrease anxiety and increase your resilience against judgmental thoughts.

MENTAL ROLE-PLAY

Socializing can be scary because we're afraid of how the other person might interact with us. Realistic visual role-playing will help us recognize the likelihood of our worst fears happening, which are low.

Consider an upcoming situation you are nervous about. This might be a job interview or a first date. Take on the role of the other person and ask yourself questions. Create a script in your mind and act this conversation out. Try a few different responses. What you will find is that your mind is reassured by the realistic things that are likely to happen.

THE POWER OF SOCIALIZATION

Socialization is incredibly important to our health, and it's easy to lose sight of that because we often spend time convincing ourselves that it's easier to live a life of isolation than to put ourselves out there. This is often a coping mechanism in response to anxiety about spending time with others. However, though it's easier to isolate than to work through our biggest socialization fears, it's necessary for our health. In fact, socialization can reduce the risk of dementia and increase mental health (*Health Benefits of Smiling*, n.d.).

Others can boost our self-esteem, provide company, and validate our feelings and experiences. Having a social network strengthens bonds to build a system of support. When you can look around you and notice that others love and care about you, it makes you realize that you are not the negative things you say to yourself.

Sometimes, it's uncomfortable to socialize because we hold onto this fear that others will "find out" who we truly are. When you feel like a failure, it can often feel like you are hiding a secret. However, the more you socialize, the more you'll learn how to feel more accepted over time. Being around others who enjoy your company will help boost confidence and provide you with reassurance that you are valued.

The following three activities can help you increase socialization and get more comfortable with the idea of being around others:

SEND A LETTER

This activity is for reaching out to someone you lost touch with. In the busyness of life, it's easy to fall out with people we once had relationships with. Take an opportunity to reconnect with others, whether it's an older relative or a friend you haven't seen for a while.

Sending a letter to an older relative is a great way to show you care. They will likely be excited and happy to hear from you.

If you don't know someone's address, send them an email or message through social media.

This activity can also be a challenge because you have no control over the situation. There is no "perfect" trigger or moment to reach out either—it requires spontaneity and initiative. You put yourself at risk for rejection, as they might simply not respond at all. This is a great form of rejection therapy that will likely end up well anyway. You might form a new friendship, and at the very least, you will show someone else that you care about them and are thinking of them.

In addition, reconnecting with an old friend can provide you with happy memories, making it easier to navigate some of your darkest past regrets (Gupta, 2022). If you look back on a certain time of your life and feel as though it was a regretful period, the person you reach out to might believe the opposite. They might remind you that this time in your life wasn't *all* bad, and in fact, you have many great memories together.

CHANGE YOUR APPEARANCE

Just like changing your physical space into something different can help change your mindset, so can changing your appearance in some way, even if it means buying a new shirt you would never have thought to try. Changing how you appear to others can help you get inspired to start a new chapter in life where you become less fearful of what other people are thinking. Ideas for changes include:

- getting a haircut or changing the color
- wearing a new outfit
- getting a new pair of glasses or trying contacts
- changing up your makeup routine
- getting a small tattoo on a visible area like your forearm

Find something that can relate to this transitional period to give you a boost into this new period in life.

JOIN A CLUB

Joining a club in something you're passionate about can help you flourish your hobby while also connecting to others with similar interests. You might find a new close friend or social group, and at the very least, you will get out of the house and interact with others. Ideas for clubs to try include:

- hobby clubs like gardening, crafting, or woodworking
- specialized sports clubs like fencing or archery

- political clubs like volunteer groups or relevant forms of activism
- knowledge-related activities like chess or book clubs

Try these things just once to help you boost your confidence and step outside of your comfort zone. There are likely online groups you can join as well if you'd prefer to ease into things.

As perfectionists, it's crucial that we step into new territory in life to break free from the habits and patterns that have kept us restricted.

CHAPTER 10
FINDING PEACE THROUGH OPEN MINDS

E ven after making progress, it can be common to slip back into old ways. Long-lasting, substantial, and unbreakable development requires that we flourish our mindset and shift perspectives.

In addition, it's easy to stop putting effort in once you see positive change. If you make it through a few projects free from perfectionist tendencies, you might think to yourself, *I finally did it!* While it's good to be proud of change and to celebrate, it can also cause us to plateau or even dive back into old ways. There has to be a level of consistency so we maintain a new mindset.

There's a common issue in the medical field of patients not finishing their round of antibiotics prescribed due to a decrease in symptoms. For example, if someone has a tooth infection, their doctor would prescribe an antibiotic, typically a pill to take between 7 and 14 days. After the third day, the patient might feel much better, so they stop taking the medicine. However, the bacteria that caused the infection is still present and can start to multiply, even building a resistance to the antibiotic, ultimately coming back. The patient then might blame the medicine for not working, not realizing it was them who didn't follow the instructions. To ensure you maintain the right mindset, you have to practice mindfulness, reflection exercises, and some of the other practical tips on a regular basis, even when you feel like you are "over" or "cured" from perfectionism. On top of this, consistent dedication can ensure you grow your mindset beyond what you ever thought possible.

Going forward, keeping an open mind is important for success. This means learning from past mistakes, facing challenges with enthusiasm, and willingly seeing things in a new way.

PERFECTIONIST REVOLUTIONS

The experience of having perfectionist thoughts can be time-consuming, exhausting, and endlessly frustrating. On a personal level, I had to get to a point where I was finally sick of the thoughts. I was beyond anxious and fearful—I was annoyed. I would look around and see that friends, family, and coworkers were able to do much with ease (or at least it looked that way). Why did I have to struggle so much? Why did I have to just be *okay* with the hand I was dealt? This kind of attitude was also frustrating, but it helped me finally get the urge to make a change.

When we feel burnt out, it's time for a revolution against our own patterns of thinking. A revolution requires that we finally realize just how serious things have gotten, and we acknowledge things *can't* continue with the way they are.

To help you foster a revolutionist mind against perfectionism, it's crucial to find evidence for negative self-perceptions and to make a habit of fact-checking feelings. Just because we've believed something up to this point does not mean it is true. Old habits and patterns sometimes feel right because they're what we're used to. Change can be uncomfortable, like trying to break in a new pair of slick leather shoes. However, once you finally find the right footing, you'll think to yourself, *How was I ever okay with the old way?*

When fact-checking your feelings, start by identifying the emotion. Use words to label them and finish with "I feel" sentences. When you're fixated on something at work that doesn't really require your attention, say to yourself, *I feel distracted by this* or *I feel unsatisfied.*

Next, consider a different perspective on this emotion. Can it wait for later? How would someone else react to this emotion? Is there a trigger that's making you feel a certain way? Experiencing emotions does not require that we act based on how they are making us feel.

Now, how can you change that feeling? Can you turn annoyance into motivation? Can you turn anger into proactivity? Can you turn sadness into a moment of peace or melancholy?

When all else fails, use visualization to kick the negative person out of your head. If you were working a customer service position and someone rudely came in and started to yell at you and the rest of the staff, you would kick them out. No one deserves to be mistreated, and we need to ensure we maintain a safe environment to keep operations running normally. Kick this voice in your mind out and visualize yourself slamming the door in its face to help you keep peace of mind.

Look at who is helping or supporting you when struggling with negative perceptions. Our environment is incredibly impactful on how we interact with our thoughts and feelings, and this includes the people we choose to have around us. If they are not helping you thrive, it might be best to reduce the time spent around them.

CREATE A MOSAIC

Do you have a broken mug that's been lying around? Do you have stacks on stacks of scrap paper? For this activity, use something old and broken and turn it into a beautiful mosaic.

To start, organize all of the pieces you have into different color categories. Next, consider what different images you can make based on the colors you have. Then, start to rearrange the pieces to create the shape. You can make a picture on a piece of paper, or you can use grout to fill in the gaps between the pieces of glass or pottery you're using. You can create something to hang on the wall, make greeting cards to send to friends, or spruce up old furniture to help you create a new environment.

The point of doing the mosaic is to help you see the way something old or broken can turn into something beautiful, and mosaics can help perfectionists who enjoy organization. It's very satisfying to create your own puzzle and come up with a creative image. This is also a very mindful activity, so every time you see your creation, you can be reminded to elicit a moment of peace.

TAKE A CLASS

There is no such thing as perfect. Even the most beautiful flower you've ever seen will eventually start to wilt. The only thing we can hope for is that it will regrow again from seed.

As perfectionists, it's hard to feel like we are good enough. Our minds are experts at always finding a way to improve. That is a quality we don't necessarily have to stifle—we just need to know how to turn it into something more practical and sustainable. One way to do this is to explore a new learning environment.

Sign up for a class in a skill you'd like to grow. Check libraries and other community resources for free classes, or consider signing up for one online. Some ideas for inspiration include:

- physical exercise classes
- creative classes
- adult sports teams
- speech or communication classes
- writing classes

Learning things on your own is important, but a class can help offer a new perspective on a subject you might have an interest in. Teachers and other classmates will challenge you and help you explore new avenues that you might not on your own.

FOSTERING CONSISTENT GROWTH

These habits are hard to break, so you might find yourself falling back into old habits. Consistent growth is the key to building a happier and healthier mindset. Use these reminders to help you keep growing when you feel you have reached a plateau:

- Once you reach a goal, ensure you take a moment to celebrate and then create new limits.
- When a setback pops into your life, try to reframe it to see it as a challenge or obstacle to overcome.
- Seek out discomfort, and if something scares you, explore that topic further until you understand why it can be so off-putting.
- Let go of old thoughts and cut off periods of rumination, reminding yourself that you don't need to know it all.

Since perfectionists tend to be results-focused, there's this sense that we just have to complete steps one to five, and then we will reach our destination.

Life feels like a set of rules that we have to complete, and then we will get what we want. This is perpetuated through our education system. Go to elementary school. When you're done, you get to go to middle and high school. Graduate with your diploma, and now you get to go to college. Go to college or trade school, and when you graduate, you can enter the workforce or go to graduate school. For most of our developmental years, there was this sense of urgency to reach an endpoint. We perpetuated this idea that once we got past points A, B, and C, we would then start to live our lives and figure out who we are.

The truth is, you're already at your destination. There's no beginning, middle, and end, especially since we never truly know when the end might be. There was a starting point, of course, but we've been alive ever since. Have you been living in the moment?

As adults, we still feel as though we just have to make it through, and then we'll get what we want. If we get married, have a kid, buy a house, and land our dream job, *then* we can finally be happy.

That's not the case. We are already on the journey, and our destination is simply to enjoy and thrive today, tomorrow, next month, and thereafter, all while living peacefully. Not every moment will be happy and filled with joy, but embracing all moments—even the stressful and chaotic— will help us live with less resistance and more clarity.

GROW FROM SEEDS

Time is a concept still not understood by the most seasoned scientists. We feel like there is never enough time, yet we can sometimes find ourselves drudging through unpleasant moments. We get stuck in the past and present, wishing we would have changed things, yet we also have a sense of urgency to make it through this period.

Growth takes time, and we can get so focused on the results that we fail to sit comfortably through that period of growth. One thing that can help you recontextualize growth is to watch a seed turn into a plant.

Head to your local garden or hardware store and purchase seeds. Set a timer to check on this every day. The process of watching something grow from seed to plant can be very beneficial in shaping your mindset.

This gives you a new perspective on time. Watching how something that's almost too small to see with the naked eye can grow into a thriving, flourishing plant is inspiring. One day, you will wake up and see a bud or a sprout and be amazed at how much can change overnight. You will look back on when it was only a seed, a reminder that time will help elicit growth.

BUILD SOMETHING

Challenge yourself to build something from scratch, like a chair, a garden bed, a crocheted scarf, or a clay pot. If you can get your hands dirty and work with creativity, you can challenge many perfectionist mindset tendencies while also having something physical to show for your efforts afterward.

Much like the seed challenge, building something is a process that you have to dedicate yourself to. Even if you make it halfway through and realize your table is too wobbly or your scarf is uneven, finish the rest. If you enjoyed the process, you can try again, creating something even better. The imperfect project serves as a reminder that life goes on even when we are not perfect! It also provides a point of comparison so you have evidence that you are capable of growth.

THE 3/30/90 CHALLENGE

This last activity is all about creating goals to give you some guidelines moving forward. As a perfectionist, creating goals is easy; it's actually following them and ensuring they're realistic that's the hard part.

This activity will help you understand how to break down goals into small parts while also helping you realize how good it feels to complete a goal.

Create a goal that you can reach in 3 days, one to reach in 30 days, and one to reach in 90 days. Each of these should be realistic, timed, and something that aligns with your overall goals and values.

All of the goals can be different, or they can connect to each other. In general, it's helpful if you have a theme to follow. Some example goals are below:

- Overall, the theme of your goals might be self-care. For the 3-day goal, you might want to purchase a journal and make your first entry. For the 30-day goal, you might want to get on a regular sleep schedule. Then, for the 90-day goal, you might want to establish a strong walking routine for your physical health.

- If you want to save money, you might have a 3-day goal of opening a savings account. Your 30-day goal is to stop spending money on anything besides necessities, like food and travel costs, such as gas. Your 90-day goal might be to save $150.

Track your progress and repeat the challenge after 90 days to notice your successes.

Overcoming perfectionism requires that we make a dedication to slowly building over time rather than expecting to see immediate results. Perfectionism pushes past realistic standards and makes us feel that if we don't have the perfect image we see in our heads, we are failures. Going forward, the more you can practice slowly building and reducing these tendencies, the sooner you will feel like things are finally *good enough*.

LET'S REVIEW

You may think that this is the part where I recap what we have learned in this book. I can see why you would think that, and we will do that in the next section, but right now I mean quite literally, Let's Review!

I hope that sharing my journey with you as I have worked to overcome my perfectionist tendencies has helped you. I hope that you have been able to see similarities between my struggles and yours and that you are now on your own path to a less stressed and more productive life.

If you have indeed found this book to be beneficial, I must ask you do to one small thing for me. Please go to Amazon and write a short review for this book so that others may feel confident buying it and beginning their own journey.

You don't have to write anything elaborate, and it absolutely doesn't have to be perfect! Any review will help me, and it may just be what helps a fellow perfectionist find their way to recovery.

You don't even have to search Amazon to find where to leave the review, simply go to reviewgoodenough.hmspub.com and you will be sent directly to the review page.

Or, even easier, scan the QR code below.

CONCLUSION

Perfectionism is common, debilitating, and hard to manage. However, it is not something you are stuck with for life. By following the 10 steps laid out through the 10 chapters, you can start to break down your most intrinsic habits to transform them into more productivity. These steps are:

- Step one: Notice perfectionist characteristics.
- Step two: Get to the root of these habits.
- Step three: Be patient with yourself and don't force immediate change.
- Step four: Change habits in small ways for more substantial growth.
- Step five: Set goals that are realistic and challenge unrealistic expectations.
- Step six: Prioritize yourself and ensure your needs are met.
- Step seven: Practice rejection to make small mistakes and failures more comfortable.

- Step eight: Stop spirals and reduce thought loops to prevent yourself from perpetuating perfectionist standards.
- Step seven: Socialize more and get back out in the world so you can recognize the true value you have.
- Step ten: Keep learning and fostering a growth mindset to prevent you from falling back into old ways.

By continually practicing and increasing awareness, you will be able to overcome your deepest perfectionist tendencies.

Finally, I want to provide you with a checklist so you can keep track of all the practical activities and exercises suggested throughout the book. This way, you can follow along in your journal to ensure you've tried everything. Highlight the ones you tried and had success with. Cross off the ones you only want to try once and circle the ones you aren't quite ready to try just yet and want to come back to. These include:

- Label the symptoms of perfectionism that have been impacting your life.
- Identify and track the way perfectionism has had effects on your day-to-day life and thought processes.
- Create goals for overcoming perfectionist tendencies.
- Increase self-reflection to gain a sense of perfectionist tendencies.

- Write a letter to your past self to help reconnect with your inner child.
- Rewrite old mistakes to help you realize they aren't as bad as they seem.
- Keep a dream journal to track some signs your deep subconscious is trying to tell you.
- Set time limits for screen usage to ensure you don't fall into a comparison trap on social media.
- Confront a mild perfectionist trigger and describe how you feel during and after.
- Try a messy hobby to help you get used to imperfection in a physical way.
- Give compliments to other people.
- Challenge yourself to try something by only making one attempt.
- Practice a body scan meditation.
- Find a way to celebrate yourself and your accomplishments.
- Break habits down into their cue, routines, and rewards so you can start to change them for higher productivity.
- Challenge yourself to swap the hand you use when brushing your teeth.
- Chunk your tasks into time blocks and set a timer to keep you on track.
- Turn negative affirmations into neutral and positive ones.
- Challenge yourself to start each day by breathing, drinking, and thinking for 15 minutes before doing anything else.
- Focus on the process rather than the journey.

- Label potential benefits of failure to make it less scary.
- Create a realistic schedule that actually appears enjoyable.
- Stop multitasking.
- Test your standards to see if you would make someone else reach these or if they are too high.
- Rework your sleep schedule for optimum energy.
- Make a goal to spend more time in nature.
- Change your space in a small way.
- Identify five different ways to say no.
- Create a chaotic outlet to help you break past perfectionist urges.
- Seek out small forms of rejection to make it more comfortable.
- Label what is in and out of your circle of control.
- Share your failure with someone else.
- Challenge yourself to try something you thought you didn't like.
- Forgive yourself for past mistakes, and then thank yourself.
- Utilize ice therapy to help snap your focus away from perfectionist urges.
- Practice mindful eating to help create normalcy around mindfulness.
- Try bug-watching to help you refocus your detail-oriented mind.
- Use a mindfulness jar to keep track of your thoughts and urges rooted in perfectionism.
- Do a blind taste test and unlock some of your mindful abilities.

- Smile at yourself in the mirror while saying encouraging phrases.
- Visualize future conversations that give you anxiety to help you realize they are unlikely to be as scary as you might think.
- Reach out to an old friend to reconnect and relive good memories.
- Find a small way to change your appearance to help you get into a new mindset.
- Join a club related to an interest you have.
- Create a mosaic and turn something old into something new.
- Take a class to help grow a skill you want to flourish.
- Grow a plant from a small seed.
- Build something with your hands.
- Try the 3/30/90-day challenge.

Keep track of the activities that help you the most and redo them as needed. Change up some of the rules and find a friend to help you with some to make them more exciting and enjoyable.

The moment you make a dedication to overcoming your perfectionism, the easier it will be to notice and rework your thoughts. You don't have to live a life constantly seeking perfection.

You are who you are—a completely unique individual with their own thoughts, opinions, and ideas that are entirely different from anyone else.

In a sense, you might maybe even say that this could be viewed as perfection in itself.

That last sentence doesn't sound quite right, and I really want to change it. But it gets the point across, so I'm going to leave it as it is. It's *good enough*!

ACKNOWLEDGMENTS

Thank you to my wife, Amanda. Without you, I would never have believed I could be a published author.

Thank you to Cece. You have an amazing talent for helping me find just the right words when I struggle with what to say.

Thank you to Jake. Your technical assistance was a lifesaver!

Thank you to Matthew, Delara, YaoYao, Lian, Fiona, Sue, Wendy, Ed, Linda, and Zsoka. Your encouragement made all the difference.

REFERENCES

Ali, S. (2022, June 19). *Why brushing your teeth with your non-dominant hand boosts brain health.* Well and Good. https://www.wellandgood.com/brushing-teeth-non-dominant-hand

Barber, N. (2021, November 10). *The benefits of failure.* Psychology Today. https://www.psychologytoday.com/us/blog/the-human-beast/202111/the-benefits-failure

Breidenthal, A., Harari, D., Steed, L., Swider, B. (2018, December 27). *The pros and cons of perfectionism, according to research.* Harvard Business Review. https://hbr.org/2018/12/the-pros-and-cons-of-perfectionism-according-to-research

Chand, S. (2017, July 10). *Social anxiety: imperfect is the new perfect.* Anxiety & Depression Association of America. https://adaa.org/learn-from-us/from-the-experts/blog-posts/consumer/social-anxiety-imperfect-new-perfect

Changing Habits. (n.d.). The Learning Center. https://learningcenter.unc.edu/tips-and-tools/changing-habits/

Chen, J., Lin, X., Luo, F., Sun, Y., Wang, J., Wang, N., Wang, Y., Zhang, X. (2022, October 10). *The relationship between perfectionism and social anxiety: a moderated mediation model.* National Library of Medicine. https://www.ncbi.nlm.nih.gov/pmc/articles/PMC9566146

Cherney, K. (2020, June 22). *Cold shower for anxiety: Does it help?* Healthline. https://www.healthline.com/health/anxiety/cold-shower-for-anxiety

Cherry, K. (2022, September 22). *What is Parkinson's law?* Verywell Mind. https://www.verywellmind.com/what-is-parkinsons-law-6674423

Cherry, K. (2023, March 1). *How multitasking affects productivity and brain health.* Verywell Mind. https://www.verywellmind.com/multitasking-2795003

Clear, J. (n.d.). *How to stop procrastinating by using the "2-minute rule."* James Clear. https://jamesclear.com/how-to-stop-procrastinating

Dawson, J., & Sleek, S. (2018, September 28). *The fluidity of time: Scientists uncover how emotions alter time perception.* Association for Psychological Science. https://www.psychologicalscience.org/observer/the-fluidity-of-time

REFERENCES

Etherson, M. (2021, February 15). *Why your perfectionism may be making you socially anxious*. Psychology Today. https://www.psychologytoday.com/us/blog/the-costs-perfectionism/202102/why-your-perfectionism-may-be-making-you-socially-anxious

Garone, S. (2021, June 10). *8 tips to meditate when you're a perfectionist*. Healthline. https://www.healthline.com/health/mind-body/how-to-meditate-when-youre-a-perfectionist

Gillete, H. (2022, March 29). *7 evidence-based strategies to manage emotional pain*. Psych Central. https://psychcentral.com/blog/how-to-deal-with-emotional-pain

Gorvett, Z. (2016, July 13). *You are surprisingly likely to have a living doppelganger*. BBC. https://www.bbc.com/future/article/20160712-you-are-surprisingly-likely-to-have-a-living-doppelganger

Gupta, S. (2022, April 19). *How to reconnect with an old friend without making it awkward*. Verywell Mind. https://www.verywellmind.com/how-to-reconnect-with-an-old-friend-without-making-it-awkward-5225930

Health benefits of social interaction. (n.d.). Mercy Care. https://www.mercycare.org/bhs/employee-assistance-program/eapforemployers/resources/health-benefits-of-social-interaction

Hof, P.R., Mulc, D., Olucha-Bordonau, F.E., Šagud, M., Šimić, G., Španić, E., Tkalčić, M., Vukšić, M., Vukić, V. (2021, May 31). *Understanding emotions: Origins and roles of the amygdala*. National Library of Medicine. https://www.ncbi.nlm.nih.gov/pmc/articles/PMC8220195

Iyengar, S., Leotti, L., & Ochsner, K. (2010, October 14). *Born to choose; the origins and value of the need for control*. National Library of Medicine. https://www.ncbi.nlm.nih.gov/pmc/articles/PMC2944661

MacDonald, A. (2011, September 12). *How to become a better perfectionist*. Harvard Health Publishing. https://www.health.harvard.edu/blog/how-to-become-a-better-perfectionist-201109123326

Martin, S. (2015, December 8). *What causes perfectionism?* Psych Central. https://psychcentral.com/blog/imperfect/2015/12/what-causes-perfectionism#1

Moore, M. (2022, September 21). *Stress and the perception of control*. Psych Central. https://psychcentral.com/stress/stress-and-the-concept-of-control

Morin, A. (2021, May 29). *What to know about perfectionist parenting*. Verywell Family. https://www.verywellfamily.com/what-to-know-about-perfectionist-parenting-4163102

Naidoo, U. (2020, October 27). *Eating well to help manage anxiety: Your questions answered*. Harvard Health Publishing. https://www.health.harvard.e-

du/blog/eating-well-to-help-manage-anxiety-your-questions-answered-
2018031413460

Perfectionism. (n.d.). Psychology Today. https://www.psychologytoday.-
com/us/basics/perfectionism

Perfectionism. (n.d.). University of Illinois at Urbana-Champaign. https://coun-
selingcenter.illinois.edu/brochures/perfectionism

Pillay, S. (2016, May 16). *Greater self-acceptance improves emotional well-being.*
Harvard Health Publishing. https://www.health.harvard.edu/blog/greater-
self-acceptance-improves-emotional-well-201605169546

Sawhney, V. (2021, June 2). *It's time to make peace with your regrets.* Harvard
Business Review. https://hbr.org/2021/06/its-time-to-make-peace-with-
your-regrets

Seltzer, L. (2008, September 10). *The path to unconditional self-acceptance.*
Psychology Today. https://www.psychologytoday.com/us/blog/evolution-
the-self/200809/the-path-unconditional-self-acceptance

Summer, J. (2023, June 20). *What is a dream journal used for?* Sleep Foundation.
https://www.sleepfoundation.org/dreams/dream-journal

Suttie, J. (2020, September 3). *Eight ways your perception of reality is skewed.*
Greater Good Magazine.
https://greatergood.berkeley.edu/article/item/eight_reasons_to_distrust_y-
our_own_perceptions

Sword, R., & Zimbardo, P. (2017, November 21). *Remorse and gratitude.*
Psychology Today. https://www.psychologytoday.com/us/blog/the-time-
cure/201711/remorse-and-gratitude

Talking to yourself: Is it normal? (2022, February 4). Cleveland Clinic.
https://health.clevelandclinic.org/is-it-normal-to-talk-to-yourself

The health benefits of smiling. (n.d.). SCL Health. https://www.s-
clhealth.org/blog/2019/06/the-real-health-benefits-of-smiling-and-
laughing

The math behind beauty: Why you're 20 percent more attractive than you think.
Huffington Post. https://www.huffpost.com/entry/the-math-behind-
beauty-wh_n_114023

Thibodeaux, W. (n.d.). *When lowering your standards is incredibly smart.* Inc.
https://www.inc.com/wanda-thibodeaux/5-times-when-lowering-your-
standards-is-most-intelligent-thing-to-do.html

Tiwary-Dennis, T. (2022, October 19). *Perfectionists: Lowering your standards can
improve your mental health.* The Washington Post. https://www.washing-
tonpost.com/wellness/2022/10/19/perfectionism-anxiety-excellence/

Voltaire. (n.d.). *Voltaire quotes.* Goodreads. https://www.goodreads.-

com/quotes/108491-perfect-is-the-enemy-of-good

Why you put things off until the last minute. (2022, December 4). Mass General Brigham. https://www.mcleanhospital.org/essential/procrastination

Made in United States
Troutdale, OR
04/18/2024

19282090R00086